W9-BFZ-582

Postmodern Art

by Stuart A. Kallen

LUCENT BOOKS
A part of Gale, Cengage Learning

Detroit • New York • San Francisco • New Haven, Conn • Waterville, Maine • London

LIBRARY OF CONGRESS CATALOGING-IN-PUBLICATION DATA

Kallen, Stuart A., 1955–
Postmodern art / by Stuart A. Kallen.
p. cm. — (Eye on art)
Includes bibliographical references and index.
ISBN 978-1-4205-0075-2 (hardcover)
1. Postmodernism—Juvenile literature. 2. Art, Modern—20th century—Juvenile literature. I. Title.
N6494.P66K35 2009
709.04—dc22
2008026599

Lucent Books
27500 Drake Rd.
Farmington Hills, MI 48331

ISBN-13: 978-1-4205-0075-2
ISBN-10: 1-4205-0075-9

Printed in the United States of America
1 2 3 4 5 6 7 12 11 10 09 08

Contents

Foreword

"Art has no other purpose than to brush aside . . . everything that veils reality from us in order to bring us face to face with reality itself."

—French philosopher Henri-Louis Bergson

Some thirty-one thousand years ago, early humans painted strikingly sophisticated images of horses, bison, rhinoceroses, bears, and other animals on the walls of a cave in southern France. The meaning of these elaborate pictures is unknown, although some experts speculate that they held ceremonial significance. Regardless of their intended purpose, the Chauvet-Pont-d'Arc cave paintings represent some of the first known expressions of the artistic impulse.

From the Paleolithic era to the present day, human beings have continued to create works of visual art. Artists have developed painting, drawing, sculpture, engraving, and many other techniques to produce visual representations of landscapes, the human form, religious and historical events, and countless other subjects. The artistic impulse also finds expression in glass, jewelry, and new forms inspired by new technology. Indeed, judging by humanity's prolific artistic output throughout history, one must conclude that the compulsion to produce art is an inherent aspect of being human, and the results are among humanity's greatest cultural achievements: masterpieces such as the architectural marvels of ancient Greece, Michelangelo's perfectly rendered statue *David*, Vincent van Gogh's visionary painting *Starry Night*, and endless other treasures.

The creative impulse serves many purposes for society. At its most basic level, art is a form of entertainment or the means for a satisfying or pleasant aesthetic experience. But art's true power lies not in its potential to entertain and delight but in its ability to enlighten, to reveal the truth, and by doing so to uplift the human spirit and transform the human race.

One of the primary functions of art has been to serve religion. For most of Western history, for example, artists were paid by the church to produce works with religious themes and subjects. Art was thus a tool to help human beings transcend mundane, secular reality and achieve spiritual enlightenment. One of the best-known, and largest-scale, examples of Christian religious art is the Sistine Chapel in the Vatican in Rome. In 1508 Pope Julius II commissioned Italian Renaissance artist Michelangelo to paint the chapel's vaulted ceiling, an area of 640 square yards (535 sq. m). Michelangelo spent four years on scaffolding, his neck craned, creating a panoramic fresco of some three hundred human figures. His paintings depict Old Testament prophets and heroes, sibyls of Greek mythology, and nine scenes from the Book of Genesis, including the Creation of Adam, the Fall of Adam and Eve from the Garden of Eden, and the Flood. The ceiling of the Sistine Chapel is considered one of the greatest works of Western art and has inspired the awe of countless Christian pilgrims and other religious seekers. As eighteenth-century German poet and author Johann Wolfgang von Goethe wrote, "Until you have seen this Sistine Chapel, you can have no adequate conception of what man is capable of."

In addition to inspiring religious fervor, art can serve as a force for social change. Artists are among the visionaries of any culture. As such, they often perceive injustice and wrongdoing and confront others by reflecting what they see in their work. One classic example of art as social commentary was created in May 1937, during the brutal Spanish civil war. On May 1 Spanish artist Pablo Picasso learned of the recent attack on the small Basque village of Guernica by German airplanes allied with fascist forces led by Francisco Franco. The German pilots had used the village for target practice, a three-hour bombing that killed sixteen hundred civilians. Picasso, living in Paris, channeled his outrage over the massacre into his painting *Guernica,* a black, white, and gray mural that depicts dismembered animals and fractured human figures whose faces are contorted in agonized expressions. Initially, critics and the public condemned the painting as an incoherent hodgepodge, but the work soon came to be seen as a powerful antiwar statement and remains an iconic symbol of the violence and terror that dominated world events during the remainder of the twentieth century.

The impulse to create art—whether painting animals with crude pigments on a cave wall, sculpting a human form from marble, or commemorating human tragedy in a mural—thus serves many purposes. It offers an entertaining diversion, nourishes the imagination and the spirit, decorates and beautifies the world, and chronicles the age. But underlying all these functions is the desire to reveal that which is obscure—to illuminate, clarify, and perhaps ennoble. As Picasso himself stated, "The purpose of art is washing the dust of daily life off our souls."

The Eye on Art series is intended to assist readers in understanding the various roles of art in society. Each volume offers an in-depth exploration of a major artistic movement, medium, figure, or profession. All books in the series are beautifully illustrated with full-color photographs and diagrams. Riveting narrative, clear technical explanation, informative sidebars, fully documented quotes, a bibliography, and a thorough index all provide excellent starting points for research and discussion. With these features, the Eye on Art series is a useful introduction to the world of art—a world that can offer both insight and inspiration.

Introduction

Beyond Modern Art

Postmodernism defines art that was created between the late 1960s and the late 1990s. To appreciate postmodernism, it is necessary to understand the modern art rejected by postmodernists. Modern art was created in the modern era after World War II when a few European and American artists became superstars. Painters such as Pablo Picasso, Piet Mondrian, Salvador Dali, and Jackson Pollock were featured not only in great museums but on the pages of popular magazines such as *Life* and *Look*. Young artists studied their brushstrokes, colors, and composition. Collectors coveted their paintings, and their company was sought by actors, authors, and politicians. Like modern rock stars, almost everyone knew their names and their work.

Modernists created paintings that made statements and used symbolic imagery. They too were rejecting art of an earlier era, specifically the painting techniques that had been valued for more than four centuries since the time of the Renaissance. The modernists threw aside concepts such as perspective, which gave subjects in paintings a three-dimensional, realistic look. They also refused to paint the exact likenesses of their subjects. For example, Picasso's cubist models were shockingly portrayed with triangular eyes, misplaced noses, and shark teeth. Dali's surrealism was inspired by dreamlike images that, while realistic, were placed in absurd, fantastic settings. Pollock's abstract expressionist paintings went beyond anything ever seen before. He produced a confusion of globs, drips, and streaks of various colors, earning him the nickname Jack the Dripper.

Modern artists were among a group of modernist writers, musicians, scholars, architects, and philosophers said to represent the progress and technological advancements of the twentieth century. Modernists most often worked in dirty cities filled with trains, automobiles, airplanes, and smoke-belching factories. They lived at a time when frightening machines of warfare killed millions and laid the countryside to waste.

In the rapidly changing twentieth century, the modernists believed that their works affirmed the power of humans over machines. Modernists believed people could create, improve, and reshape their environment with the aid of scientific knowledge, technology, and experimentation. In their pursuit of progress modernists challenged every aspect of life, including the arts, religion, philosophy, politics, and business. They wanted to advance humanity by replacing traditions they believed were standing in the way of progress.

Challenging Modernism

At its inception, modern art was seen as provocative, radical, and outrageous. However, by the mid-twentieth century, modernist painters had been widely accepted. Their works were reproduced on posters and in books and magazines. Their once unique visual concepts were widely imitated by advertisers, fashion designers, and graphic artists. Modernism had become mainstream culture. Buyers eagerly purchased modernist paintings not for their artistic importance but for their investment value.

New art movements are always led by those who reject the accepted standards. Modernism was a rebellion against the conservative concepts of nineteenth-century art. By the late 1960s, however, modernism was seen as the established order.

By the mid-twentieth century works by modernist painters had been reproduced on books, posters, and even fashion, as was the case with artist Andy Warhol's "souper dress," modeled after his famous 1960s painting.

New artists wished to distance themselves from modernism, and so the postmodern movement was born.

Postmodern simply means "after modern," but it is often interpreted to mean antimodern. Where modernists hoped to discover universal truths, postmodernism aimed to challenge them. Whereas most modern art could be put into categories such as cubism, expressionism, or surrealism, postmodern artists rejected such limitations. They preferred instead to combine any and every visual style. The postmodernists embraced so-called low art forms such as commercials, magazines, and graphic arts. They saw stark artistic beauty in trash or industrial waste, known as found art. The modern televised media also provided inspiration with its nonstop barrage of incongruent and disconnected images. As such, a postmodern piece might include words from an ad, images from the Renaissance, garbage found in a gutter, and a bank of video monitors showing contrasting images.

With a wide variety of tools and images, postmodernists were free to combine any elements or styles in a work. They could also use their work to make humorous, ironic, satirical, or playful statements, a concept referred to as *jouissance*, French for "pleasure."

Most postmodern artists were members of the first television generation and as a result grew into adulthood realizing the absurdity of modern culture.

Good Culture, Bad Culture

Postmodern art rejects the modernist view of art as a serious endeavor to be pursued only by a few talented individuals. By doing so, postmodernists liberated arts and artists. This is not to say that postmodernism has not generated a fair share of criticism. As photographer and critic David Bates notes: "For the cultural conservatives, postmodern culture was [seen

as] destroying the important distinctions within society about what was good culture (classical music, theatre, painting, novels) and what was not (pop, television, photography and video, tabloids and celebrity magazines)."[1]

Perhaps this breakdown between old concepts and new is a result of the television and digital age. Most postmodern artists were of the first television generation, baby boomers who grew up watching TV. As children they viewed gruesome images of the Vietnam War on the evening news mixed with commercials for shiny new cars and gleaming kitchen appliances. While most people considered this jumble of images a normal part of daily life, postmodernists viewed them as absurd. They found similarly ridiculous situations and images everywhere in modern culture. Homeless people slept in the streets beneath luminous skyscrapers; wealthy, educated businessmen cheated the public with rapacious greed; and corrupt politicians lectured the public about law and order. As author Jonathan Selwood writes in *The Pinball Theory of the Apocalypse*, "People experience truly ludicrous situations every day of their lives, and yet instead of confronting them, they choose to put on blinders and ignore them."[2]

Rather than trying to make sense of this senseless world, postmodernists celebrated the preposterous through art. In this way they called attention to the mindless messages of the media and attempted to remove society's blinders.

While it may seem confusing to make a point by being pointless, postmodernism dominated the art world in the last quarter of the twentieth century. As the postmodern age fades into the digital age of the twenty-first century, the impact of the postmodernists is clear. Digital artists draw their inspiration from a nearly infinite variety of styles. These include television, films, celebrity culture, and classical painting genres. They combine artistic beauty, scathing social commentary, and playful visuals. Conceivably this is post-postmodernism. Whatever it is called, artists will continue to take their inspiration from what they see around them. And as the postmodernists proved, the artistic muse comes in many shapes and forms.

1

Roots of Postmodernism

The history of twentieth-century art has been divided into neat categories by scholars, philosophers, and critics. These distinctions make people aware, for example, that the cubist era began in the spring of 1907 when Pablo Picasso created the revolutionary masterpiece *Young Ladies of Avignon*. In the painting, Picasso depicted his female models in distorted perspective, uneven angles, chunky blocks, and geometric shapes. History is often messy, however, and in reality artistic creativity is hard to pin down. Picasso's cubism was inspired by the angular faces carved into ancient African ceremonial masks. Therefore, cubism was inspired by nameless artists from another era.

The same concept applies to postmodernism. Art critics say that the postmodernist movement incubated in the late 1960s, a time of massive student uprisings against the Vietnam War, riots in the streets, and a gaping chasm between the older generation and the young. Millions of people were rejecting the modern technological society that the previous generation celebrated. A break in the modern world had clearly occurred, and as modernism fell away, postmodernism replaced it. But just as African masks inspired Picasso to create a new style, the postmodernists were inspired by extremely important art movements in the early twentieth century. Without these aspects of modernism, there would be no postmodernism.

Picasso's Influence

Postmodern artists combine several types of art into one genre, or style. They construct pictures by gluing pieces of cloth, newspaper, written words, photographs, and other objects to the surface of a painting, a technique known as collage and montage. They assemble found objects such as trash, clothing,

Picasso's work titled *Guitar* became the first piece of art to be assembled out of separate pieces and opened the door to a new form of artwork called constructed sculpture.

and household items into assemblage art. They use dance, music, theatrics, and newer forms of media, such as computers, in performance art. They also use pranks and humor to mock or criticize popular culture, politics, and social traditions. Some of these facets of postmodern art, however, are not unique, and in fact, their roots may be traced to Pablo Picasso.

In addition to inventing the cubist painting style, Picasso was the first to use collage in a work of art. In 1912 he made *Still Life with Chair Caning* by pasting a piece of printed oilcloth that resembled woven chair caning onto a canvas. He added the letters "JOU" (a pun on the French word for "play") cut from the masthead of the French newspaper *Le Journal.* Finally he framed the entire oval picture with a piece of rope.

Around the same time, Picasso created the first of what is now called constructed sculpture. *Guitar* is an angular, cubist version of a guitar made from sheet metal and wire. Unlike any other previous sculpture, *Guitar* was not cast from metal or carved from a single block of wood or stone. Instead it was assembled out of separate elements. This work opened the door for the twentieth-century constructed sculpture and assemblage movements.

Readymades

Picasso's cubist paintings also acted as inspiration for others, including French artist Marcel Duchamp. In 1912 Duchamp painted the cubist masterpiece *Nude Descending a Staircase, No. 2.* Going beyond Picasso's flat, motionless images, Duchamp portrayed an abstract figure in a series of images overlaid or superimposed over one another. Inspired by stop-motion photography, a medium that was popular at the time, Duchamp's distorted figures give the impression of movement.

When Duchamp submitted *Nude Descending a Staircase* to the 1913 Armory Show in New York City, it created a scandal. Americans were accustomed to realistic art and had little exposure to the European cubist phenomenon. The art critic for the *New York Times* wrote that the painting resembled an explosion in a shingle factory. Stung by this experience, Duchamp denounced the idea of artistic genres and ideals of beauty. After visiting an

Marcel Duchamp's work *Bicycle Wheel* consisted of objects for which he coined the phrase "assisted readymades." This resulted in the concept that anything could be considered art if it was displayed as such.

aviation exhibition and viewing airplanes, he told his friend, Romanian sculptor Constantin Brancusi, "Painting's washed up. Who will ever do anything better than that propeller?"[3]

In the pursuit of mechanical beauty, Duchamp combined everyday objects into an unusual work of art. He drilled a hole in the seat of a plain white wooden stool and attached a bicycle wheel on its front fork. Commenting on the pleasure he received from spinning the wheel, Duchamp later said, "I enjoyed looking at it, just as I enjoy looking at the flames dancing in a fireplace."[4]

When World War I began in 1914, Duchamp moved to New York City to avoid being drafted into the French army. Much to the artist's surprise, he found that he had become a celebrity due to the *Nude Descending a Staircase* controversy. When he showed *Bicycle Wheel* to several art patrons, they

Duchamp's Readymades

Marcel Duchamp displayed everyday objects as works of art called readymades. The Museum of Modern Art (MOMA) explains the concepts behind the readymade Bicycle Wheel*:*

Bicycle Wheel is Duchamp's first Readymade, a class of artworks that raised fundamental questions about artmaking and, in fact, about art's very definition. . . . Duchamp was not the first to kidnap everyday stuff for art; the Cubists had done so in collages, which, however, required aesthetic judgment in the shaping and placing of materials. The Readymade, on the other hand, implied that the production of art need be no more than a matter of selection—of choosing a preexisting object. In radically subverting earlier assumptions about what the artmaking process entailed, this idea had enormous influence on later artists, particularly . . . in the 1950s and 1960s.

The components of *Bicycle Wheel*, being mass-produced, are anonymous, identical or similar to countless others. In addition, the fact that this version of the piece is not the original seems inconsequential, at least in terms of visual experience. Duchamp claimed to like the work's appearance, "to feel that the wheel turning was very soothing." Even now, *Bicycle Wheel* retains an absurdist visual surprise.

The Museum of Modern Art, *MOMA Highlights*. New York: Museum of Modern Art, 2004, p. 87.

named the individual parts of the work "Readymades." This name could apply to any object the artist purchased "as a sculpture already made." When Duchamp modified these objects, for example, by mounting the wheel on the stool, he called them "Assisted Readymades."[5]

Although they were created in a spirit of playful humor, Duchamp's readymades challenged basic concepts of art. Throughout history, artists were expected to possess uncommon talent and skill. When Duchamp bolted a bicycle wheel onto a stool and called it art, he made a statement that anything could be art if it was displayed as such. This rejection of art came to be called anti-art. It required the creator to build the work without a preconceived vision, artistic inspiration, or sense of aesthetics (appreciation of art or beauty). As Duchamp said, "You have to approach something with an indifference, as if you have no aesthetic emotion. The choice of Readymades is always based on visual indifference and, at the same time, on the total absence of good or bad taste."[6]

A Mass Media Explosion

Unbeknownst to Duchamp, there were others, known as Dadaists, creating anti-art on their own terms. Dadaism began in Zurich, Switzerland, in 1916 during the bloody, senseless destruction of World War I. Dadaists believed that the unprecedented slaughter was a result of a society that worshiped machines and technology. This misplaced reverence for science and industry resulted in the horrors of mechanized warfare—tanks, machine guns, poison gas, and hand grenades—used for the first time with brutal efficiency in World War I.

Dadaists believed that the pillars of society, such as law, faith, language, economy, education, and traditional gender roles, had failed to prevent the unprecedented destruction of the war. They also held that society had been tricked into this illogical behavior by a new form of communication. Leah Dickerman explains in *Dada*:

> Perhaps most important for the Dada movement was the emergence of a modern media culture, a development

The Dada Manifesto

On July 14, 1916, Hugo Ball released "The Dada Manifesto," which explained in abstract and somewhat confusing terms the Dada movement he helped invent:

Dada is a new tendency in art. . . . Dada comes from the dictionary. It is terribly simple. In French it means "hobby horse." In German it means "good-by," "Get off my back," "Be seeing you sometime." In Romanian: "Yes, indeed, you are right, that's it. But of course, yes, definitely, right." And so forth.

An international word. Just a word, and the word a movement. Very easy to understand. Quite terribly simple. . . . Dada psychology, dada Germany cum indigestion . . . dada literature, dada bourgeoisie, and yourselves, honored poets.

. . . Dada world war without end, dada revolution without beginning. . . .

How does one achieve eternal bliss? By saying dada. How does one become famous? By saying dada. With a noble gesture and delicate propriety. Till one goes crazy. Till one loses consciousness. How can one get rid of everything that smacks of journalism, worms, everything nice and right, blinkered, moralistic?

. . . By saying dada. Dada is the world soul, dada is the pawnshop. Dada is the world's best lily-milk soap. . . . I don't want words that other people have invented. All the words are other people's inventions. I want my own stuff, my own rhythm, and vowels and consonants too, matching the rhythm and all my own.

Hugo Ball, "Dada Manifesto," July 14, 1916. www.391.org/manifestos/hugoball_dadamanifesto.htm.

catalyzed by the experience of war. Propaganda poster campaigns with coordinated messages were deployed on a massive scale. The development of communication technology—radio, cinema, and newsreels, and a new photo-illustrated press—fostered the flow of information from battlefront to home front. The science of wireless telegraphy . . . led to a surge in public broadcasting and the mass production of "radio music boxes" in its wake. Newsreels, which first appeared in 1911, captured battle action . . . and nurtured the emergence of a commercial film industry. . . . These wartime developments triggered a postwar mass-media explosion. . . . For the individual observer, there was a threshold jump in the number of images and amount of print material circulated in the public sphere.[7]

A New Tendency in Art

Dadaists utilized the new communications methods to express their loss of faith in society. German poet Hugo Ball, who founded the Dada movement, believed that since reason, logic, and science had led to the insanity of war, the only sane reaction was to promote artistic anarchy with irrational statements and illogical anti-art. Early Dada poet Romanian Tristan Tzara described his view of the movement: "The beginnings of Dada were not the beginnings of an art, but those of a disgust."[8]

Switzerland was neutral during the war, and many painters, poets, and performers fled to Zurich to avoid the bloodshed. Ball saw an opportunity to bring these like-minded young artists and war resisters together. In February 1916 he opened a nightclub, the Cabaret Voltaire, and within a week it filled with a group of nonconformists who formed the core of the Dada movement. They included Tzara; Ball's wife, poet, singer, and dancer Emily Hennings; French-German sculptor and painter Jean (Hans) Arp; and German poet, writer, and drummer Richard Huelsenbeck.

Arp created two of the earliest Dada works of art, *According to the Laws of Chance* and *Arrangement According to the Law of Chance*. As the titles suggests, Arp composed these collages by chance. He dropped torn bits of paper onto the floor in a random method and pasted them onto a piece of paper more or less as they had fallen. As the Web site for the New York Museum of Modern Art (MOMA) explains:

> This elegantly composed collage of torn-and-pasted paper is a playful, almost syncopated [musically rhythmic] composition in which uneven squares seem to dance within the space. . . . Arp [developed this] method of making collages . . . in order to create a

Jean (Hans) Arp's *According to the Laws of Chance* became one of the first pieces of Dada art. This work inspired other artists, such as Kurt Schwitters, to follow the Dada method in the coming years.

> work that was free of human intervention and closer to nature. The incorporation of chance operations was a way of removing the artist's will from the creative act . . . so as to divorce his work from [what Arp called] "the life of the hand."[9]

Arp's work inspired German poet, painter, sculptor, and collage artist Kurt Schwitters in Hanover. Schwitters's first collage, *Hansi*, strongly resembles Arp's work. Soon after, however, he began to follow his own path, making assemblages from scraps of found materials. These included tram tickets, coupons, postage stamps, beer labels, candy wrappers, newspaper clippings, fabric swatches, and rusty nails. Schwitters felt that these items reflected the flux, or changeability, of modern society. Schwitters called one collage a Merz picture, and afterward referred to all his work as Merz, which he said meant "a principle of openness toward everything."[10] One such piece, *Merz Column*, consists of a square column covered with words and images from newspapers and magazines. Various items sit atop the column, including a baby-doll head, a cow horn, a laurel branch, some crocheted cloth, and various items made from plaster, metal, and wood.

"The Dada Manifesto"

Schwitters was also a poet who used collage methods to construct poems, putting together random words to create a single piece. Tzara, who pioneered this technique, explained that to write Dada poetry an artist should: "Take a newspaper. Take a pair of scissors. Choose an article. . . . Cut out the article. Then cut out each of the words that make up this article and put them in a bag. Shake it gently. Then take out the scraps one after the other in the order in which they left the bag. Copy [onto paper]. . . . The poem will be like you."[11]

Tzara's technique was used by Ball to create a manifesto, or declaration of principles, policies, and objectives meant to introduce Dada philosophy to a mass audience. By stringing together seemingly incongruous phrases, made-up words, and poetic symbols, "The Dada Manifesto" makes three main points, according to the Electro-Acoustic Music Web site dedicated to Dada composers:

1. Dada is international in perspective and seeks to bridge differences.
2. Dada is antagonistic toward established society . . . and
3. Dada is a new tendency in art that seeks to change conventional attitudes and practices in aesthetics, society, and morality.[12]

Ball also published several magazines with Dada poetry and art. Meanwhile, Tzara was producing his own Dada poems and manifestos. One of his books, with the unusual title *The First Celestial Adventure of Mr. Fire Extinguisher*, was a script from a performance piece given at the Cabaret Voltaire. This book, with characters named Mr. Fire Extinguisher and Mr. Shriekshriek, was sent to Duchamp in New York. It was the first time the readymade artist saw the word Dada. Although Duchamp is today associated with the founding of Dadaism, he insisted for many years that the crowd in Zurich did not influence him: "It was parallel, if you wish. . . . [My work] wasn't Dada, but it was in the same spirit, without, however, being in the Zurich spirit."[13]

Mr. Mutt's Fountain

Despite his denials, Duchamp is forever associated with Dada due to his readymade piece *Fountain*. The work is a urinal the artist bought at a plumbing supply store, R.L. Mott Iron Works, on New York's Fifth Avenue. Duchamp took the urinal to his studio, turned it 90 degrees from its normal position, so the rounded front jutted up into the air, and wrote "R. Mutt, 1917" on it.

Duchamp was a board member of a group called the Society of Independent Artists. He entered *Fountain* in its first annual exhibition in April 1917, under the pseudonym R. Mutt. Although the group's policy was to display any artwork submitted, it refused to put *Fountain* in the show. Some board members believed it was immoral and vulgar while others said it was plagiarism since it was a plain piece of plumbing. Duchamp responded to these charges in the Dada magazine *Blind Man*:

> Now Mr. Mutt's fountain is not immoral, that is absurd. . . . It is a fixture which you see every day in plumbers' show windows. Whether Mr. Mutt made the fountain with his own hands or not has no importance. He CHOSE it. He took an article of life, placed it so that its useful significance disappeared under the new title and point of view—created a new thought for that object. As for plumbing, that is absurd. The only works of art America has produced are her plumbing and her bridges.[14]

The rejection of *Fountain* caused a sensation covered extensively by the New York press. The widespread shock and controversy became part of the Dada joke. By its overreaction to the sight of a common plumbing fixture, society was made to look ridiculous, much more so than the artist who attempted to display it.

Duchamp continued in the Dadaist spirit of revolt against art and morality. In 1919 he created *L.H.O.O.Q.* by defacing one of the world's most revered paintings, *Mona Lisa*, by Leonardo da Vinci. *L.H.O.O.Q.* was a cheap postcard-sized reproduction of *Mona Lisa*, upon which Duchamp drew a mustache and a goatee. According to the Duchamp World Community Web site, "The 'readymade' . . . is one of the most well known acts of degrading a famous work of art."[15]

The End of Dada

Duchamp continued to produce thought-provoking work until his death in 1968. However, by the early 1920s many Dadaists moved on to other art movements. In Paris, Dadaist André Breton felt the movement was at turns either too scathing and negative or too silly, what he called "Dada Buffoonery."[16] Breton began promoting a new style, surrealism. This art concept was based on dreamlike images that ran through Breton's mind in the moments before falling asleep. The images might

"I'm Not Aware of What I'm Doing"

On August 8, 1949, Life *magazine ran an article on Jackson Pollock along with photos of him at work. The article, "Is He the Greatest Living Painter in the United States?" is excerpted below:*

"My painting does not come from the easel," [Pollock explains]. "I need the resistance of a hard surface." Working on the floor gives him room to scramble around the canvas, attacking it from the top, the bottom or the side (if his pictures can be said to have a top, a bottom or a side) as the mood suits him. In this way, "I can . . . literally be in the painting." He surrounds himself with quart cans of aluminum paint and many hues of ordinary household enamel. Then, starting anywhere on the canvas, he goes to work. Sometimes he dribbles the paint on with a brush. Sometimes he scrawls it on with a stick, scoops it with a trowel or even pours it on straight out of the can. . . . Cigarette ashes and an occasional dead bee sometimes get in the picture inadvertently.

"When I am in my painting," says Pollock, "I'm not aware of what I'm doing." To find out what he has been doing he stops and contemplates the picture during what he calls his "get acquainted" period. Once in a while a lifelike image appears in the painting by mistake. But Pollock cheerfully rubs it out because the picture must retain "a life of its own." Finally, after days of brooding and doodling, Pollock decides the painting is finished, a deduction few others are equipped to make.

Quoted in *Life*, "Is He the Greatest Living Painter in the United States?" August 8, 1945. www.theslidepro jector.com/art1/art1primarysources/1949lifearticle.html.

Jackson Pollock dribbles sand on one of his works while in his studio. Pollock's works became known as action paintings because of the dance movements he used to create them.

be of realistic, common objects, but were viewed in absurd, otherworldly settings. Spanish artist Salvador Dali created some of the most famous surrealist imagery, painting melted watches draped over tree branches and disjointed body parts in barren landscapes.

Although the Dada era was over, the style influenced a generation of American artists who began their careers after World War II. Foremost among them was Wyoming-born painter Jackson Pollock, who created what came to be called "action paintings" for the ferocious dance the artist performed to create them. Pollock began a work by tacking a large piece of unframed canvas to the floor. Picking up buckets of thick liquid paint called gloss enamel, he danced and jumped around the canvas. He either poured various colors onto the medium or dripped and splashed the paint with sticks, trowels, knives, hardened brushes, and turkey basters. As it dried, he deliberately added sand, broken glass, nails, coins, and even cigarette butts to the sticky paint.

Pollock's manner of action painting was based on what Dadaists and surrealists called automatism. This theory supposes that artists can create works based on unconscious thoughts, revelations, and moods rather than through a planned process. Pollock's use of this technique was described by Kirk Varnedoe, the late curator of painting and sculpture at MOMA:

> When you look at [a Pollock painting], it's clear that no matter how long it took him to paint this picture, he never thought twice during the whole time he was painting it. There is a family of marks, hooks, commas, scythe-like marks, long loops and sinews that set up a rhythm. And that rhythm runs across the length of the canvas like a kind of stampede. It's clear that he got onto something, it got a hold of him, and he let it rip across the surface of the canvas.[17]

Pollock's drip paintings created a sensation, and the artist was featured in a number of popular magazines. In 1949 *Life* posed the question "Is he the greatest living painter?"[18] In 1956 *Time* labeled Pollock "Jack the Dripper." Although Pollock disdained such publicity, it is clear he redefined how artwork was created. His move away from the easel, brush, and palette liberated artists from any and all artistic traditions. Pollock also presented a romantic view of the artist as someone who was defined by his work and believed that painting was a way of life.

Shoes, Hens, and Goats: Abstract Expressionism

Pollock belonged to what was called the New York School of painters, consisting of Americans and Europeans based in New York City. (In this usage, *school* is not a learning institution but is used to define a group of people who share a similar artistic philosophy and style.) Their work came to be known as abstract expressionism, and in addition to Pollock, other abstract expressionists include Willem de Kooning, Franz Kline, and Mark Rothko. These painters are categorized into two groups. Some, such as Rothko, are called color-field artists because they painted simple, unified blocks of color onto a canvas. Others, like Pollock and de Kooning, are action painters who used automatic art techniques to create abstract works with no definable subject matter.

A third type of abstract expressionism is seen in the works of Texas-born artist Robert Rauschenberg. In the 1950s Rauschenberg created a series of works, called "Combines," that blend abstract artwork with various objects. These pieces of assemblage art, created from preserved animals, large objects, and commercial photography, are reminiscent of works by Schwitters. For example, the unusual materials in a Rauschenberg piece called *Untitled*, created in 1954, are described by New York's Metropolitan Museum of Art as "oil, pencil, crayon, paper, canvas, fabric, newspaper, photographs, wood, glass, mirror, tin, cork and found painting with pair of painted leather shoes, dried grass, and Dominique hen mounted on wood structure on five casters."[19]

Other Rauschenberg assemblages included items such as the stuffed head of a real Angora goat, pieces of rubber tires, soda bottles, and a bald eagle covered in black paint. Commenting on Rauschenberg's use of found materials, *New York Times* art critic Michael Kimmelman writes, "It is largely, if not exclusively, thanks to Robert Rauschenberg that Americans since the 1950's have come to think that art can be made out of anything, exist anywhere, last forever or just for a moment and serve almost any purpose or no purpose at all except to suggest that the stuff of life and the stuff of art are ultimately one and the same."[20]

Familiar Images

By the mid-1950s New York artists were searching for a style to follow abstract expressionism. Jasper Johns, who was extremely interested in Duchamp's readymades and the Dada irreverence for traditional art forms, believed he found an answer. Johns began creating paintings with familiar images such

American artist Jasper Johns used familiar images in his artwork, such as the U.S. flag in this piece titled *Flag Above White with Collage, 1955.* Johns was searching for a style of art to follow abstract expressionism.

as words, numbers, and flags, as in *White Flag*. This 1955 piece features an American flag constructed from tinted beeswax (called encaustic), newsprint, fabric, and charcoal.

In the years that followed, Johns created several more American flags along with works containing targets, numbers, letters, maps, rulers, beer cans, and puzzle pictures. Like Pollock, Johns believed that the act of creation was as important as the work or art itself. Regarding the simplicity of the subject matter, Johns stated: "There may or may not be an idea, and the meaning may just be that the painting exists."[21]

In the early 1960s artists David Hockney, Richard Hamilton, and Roy Lichtenstein took the idea of using familiar images one step further. Using images drawn from popular mass culture, these artists created popular art or pop art. These images were meant to have a broader appeal than the academic and obscure images of the abstract expressionists. Hamilton's early work features abstract images of American automobiles, while Lichtenstein painted giant cartoons similar to those found in comic books.

Hockney created images based on his travels to Los Angeles in the 1960s. For example, *A Bigger Splash* shows in simple geometric patterns a diving board, a swimming pool, a typical California ranch house, and two palm trees. Bright blue dominates the painting in the pool and the sky. The color was applied in several layers with a paint roller typically used for painting walls.

Hockney rejected the pop art label because he wanted his work to be taken seriously. Compared to the era's most famous pop artist, Andy Warhol, Hockney's work is much more painterly, that is, typical of a good painter. Warhol, on the other hand, embraced crass commercialism and a determined lack of meaning in his work.

Warhol Paints Campbell's Soup Cans

Warhol was a commercial artist in New York City in 1962 when a friend suggested that he make a painting of something very common, something everyone would recognize, "like a can of Campbell's soup."[22] A few months later Warhol displayed thiry-two oversize, realistic paintings of Campbell's soup cans in a Los Angeles gallery. Some canvases featured a single can, others had one hundred cans of different flavors, such as black bean soup, bean and bacon, and vegetable. Critics panned the show for its trite subject matter, while the gallery owner next door stacked real cans of Campbell's soup in the window, offering to sell the "artwork" to collectors for twenty-nine cents. Despite the scorn and negative reviews, the publicity made Warhol an international pop art sensation.

After achieving instant fame, Warhol set up an art studio in New York and named it the "Factory." As the name implies, he used the Factory to mass-produce art. Abandoning paintbrushes, he created silk screen portraits of famous people such as actress Marilyn Monroe, former first lady Jackie Kennedy, and Chinese dictator Mao Zedong. Using garish pinks, reds, greens, and yellows, the portraits, according to the Andy Warhol Homepage, "can be taken as comments on the banality, harshness, and ambiguity of American culture."[23]

Andy Warhol became instantly famous in 1962 after he exhibited thirty-two paintings of Campbell's soup cans in a Los Angeles gallery.

Silk screening allowed Warhol to mass-produce images of supermarket products such as Coke bottles, Brillo Soap Pads, Mott's Apple Juice, and Heinz Tomato Ketchup. In another act meant to mock the concept of art, Warhol held a "Do-It-Yourself" show in which pictures were half colored and patrons were given crayons and colored pencils and encouraged to finish the work.

Warhol's work was Dadaism taken to a logical extreme in a modern world that had come to equate manufactured products with art. He also made so-called "low art" acceptable. Pop art, along with Dada, abstract expressionism, and other modernist forms, laid the groundwork for the postmodern era that followed.

2

Conceptual Art

Great art often makes viewers think and question the images presented to them. This was particularly true in the twentieth century. From Picasso to Duchamp to Rauschenberg, viewers were often puzzled by what the artist was saying with his artwork. This resulted in millions of words written by psychiatrists, philosophers, critics, and scholars. In fact, an entire industry developed in the twentieth century to explain, justify, or condemn works of cubism, Dadaism, or abstract expressionism.

Whatever was written, artists continued to follow their vision, keeping their intentions to themselves, and leaving the analysis to others. As Ursula Meyer writes in *Conceptual Art*, "The function of the critic and the function of the artist has been traditionally divided; the artist's concern was the production of the work and the critic's was its evaluation and interpretation."[24]

The relationship between artist and critic began to break down in the late 1950s with the advent of conceptual art. Rather than let a middleman, such as a critic, define art for the public, the conceptual artist explained his or her ideas with words or written instructions. While these too were often baffling, the concepts and intentions defined by the artist came to play an important role in the total artwork.

The Machine Makes the Art

American artist Sol LeWitt conceived of over twelve hundred large wall paintings that were executed by others who used his artistic statements to create the works. His paintings featured geometric designs such as stars, rectangles, and stripes. Some were drab and neutral, others bursting with color. The directions to wall painting *No. 766* provide insight into LeWitt's work. He provided vague directions to draftspersons and painters, stating simply, "Twenty-one isometric cubes of varying sizes each with color ink washes superimposed."[25] While this may sound dry and uninteresting, when the painting was recreated on the walls of the Whitney Museum of American Art in New York in 2000, the colorful, mural-sized concept took teams of

American artist Sol LeWitt directed several teams of painters and designers with verbal instructions to finish his painting *No. 766* on the walls of the Whitney Museum of American Art in New York in 2000. Because of its placement, the work was eventually painted over.

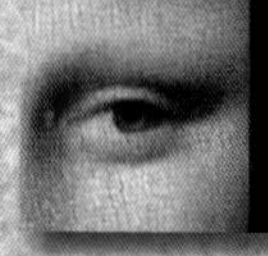

"Not Necessarily Logical"

In 1967 pioneering conceptual artist Sol LeWitt described his work in an Artforum *article, "Paragraphs on Conceptual Art," excerpted below:*

I will refer to the kind of art in which I am involved as conceptual art. . . . This kind of art is not [about] theories; it is intuitive [instinctive and spontaneous], it is involved with all types of mental processes and it is purposeless. It is usually free from the dependence on the skill of the artist as a craftsman. It is the objective of the [conceptual] artist . . . to make his work mentally interesting to the spectator, and therefore usually he would want it to become emotionally dry. There is no reason to suppose, however, that the conceptual artist is out to bore the viewer. . . .

Conceptual art is not necessarily logical. . . . Logic may be used to camouflage the real intent of the artist, to lull the viewer into the belief that he understands the work. . . .

The ideas need not be complex. Most ideas that are successful are ludicrously simple. Successful ideas generally have the appearance of simplicity because they seem inevitable. In terms of ideas the artist is free even to surprise himself. . . .

What the work of art looks like isn't too important. It has to look like something if it has physical form. No matter what form it may finally have it must begin with an idea.

Sol LeWitt, "Paragraphs on Conceptual Art," *Artforum*, June 1967. www.ddooss.org/articulos/idiomas/Sol_Lewitt.htm.

French artist Yves Klein's *Arthropométries of the Blue Age* was considered one his most controversial pieces because he used nude women as "living brushes" to create the work.

paintings to amused buyers after bargaining shrewdly over the price. Commenting on the meaning of Klein's concept in *The Triumph of Anti-Art*, professor and art critic Thomas McEvilley writes, "*The Void* was a derisive [mocking] critique of the art object, the art business, and the role of the artist."[31]

Klein's subsequent paintings were not invisible but only existed as piles of ashes. In 1960 he created about a hundred "Fire Paintings," using a flamethrower as "paint" to dematerialize his canvases. Using another technique, Klein created *One Minute Fire Painting* by lighting sixteen firecrackers attached to a blue monochrome panel.

One of Klein's most controversial pieces was called *Anthropométries of the Blue Age*. Wearing a tuxedo and white gloves, the artist directed the creation of work without ever touching the materials. At the public event, held in a gallery, a string ensemble played *Monotone-Silence Symphony*, written by Klein. The song consisted of one chord, a D-major, played for twenty minutes, followed by an equal period of silence. Artwork was created by women who applied blue paint, called International Klein Blue, to their nude bodies. At the instruction of the artist, the women rolled around on large sheets of paper. In this manner, Klein produced two hundred body paintings, or anthropometries, made with "living brushes."[32] These works were viewed as parodies of traditional figure paintings in which artists painted nude models.

City Streets as Art Spaces

Klein died of a heart attack at the age of thirty-four. At the time of his death in 1962, many Europeans considered him the most important French artist since World War II. However, many conceptualists had moved away from the idea of an art gallery as an exhibition space even for conceptual art. The new idea was to execute art concepts in city streets among average people, a notion advanced in Amsterdam by Stanley Brouwn. In 1960 Brouwn announced that all shoe-store windows in the city constituted an exhibition of his work. Those who wanted to view Brouwn's "art" simply needed to look into the window of any shoe store.

Brouwn later became fascinated with measurement and direction. In 1962 he created *This Way Brouwn* by stopping random pedestrians and asking them to draw maps to various points in the city, such as museums, tram stops, and stores. The hastily scrawled maps were to include estimated kilometers to

Artists Jeanne-Claude and Christo posed for a photo during the work of art *The Gates, Central Park, New York City, 1979–2005.*

the destination, or even the number of footsteps required to walk there. The artist called each map *This Way Brouwn*. By 1969 Brouwn had collected five hundred such maps, which he displayed in an exhibit. This piece was meant to demonstrate the ways in which people perceive and measure urban space.

The idea of using city streets for art was taken in a different direction by Bulgarian-born, American artist Christo and his French wife Jeanne-Claude. In 1958, Christo developed the concept of drawing attention to an object by hiding it. To do so, Christo wrapped everyday objects, such as a wine bottle, a pile of magazines, a nightstand, a motorcycle, an even a Volkswagen, in sheets of fabric. By hiding the object, it became a piece of art worthy of consideration and study.

In 1961, Christo and Jeanne-Claude applied the idea of wrapping to an outdoor artwork called *Dockside Packages* at Cologne Harbor on the Rhine River. Christo and Jeanne-Claude borrowed materials from the dockworkers and wrapped tarps around a stack of oil barrels and secured the material with rope. The work stood for two weeks and then was dismantled.

In 1962, Christo and Jeanne-Claude again took their work to the city streets. They illegally closed off a narrow Paris street, Rue Visconti, for eight hours using 240 oil barrels to build a barricade. This work, *Wall of Barrels, Iron Curtain*, was meant to protest the Berlin Wall, or Iron Curtain, that the Soviet Union had built in East Germany to prevent citizens of communist Eastern Europe from migrating to democratic Western Europe. Christo had recently escaped from communism. He traveled from his home in Bulgaria to Prague (another communist country) and from Prague, he escaped into non-communist Vienna, Austria. Christo also wanted to draw attention to the restrictions Soviets imposed upon the citizens of communist countries. Christo and Jeanne-Claude's Iron Curtain created a major traffic jam that halted movement for thousands of Parisians. Although Rue Visconti is little more than 12 feet (4 m.) wide, it is an important thoroughfare and the art piece tied up traffic for three hours.

Temporary Monuments

In 1964, Christo and Jeanne-Claude moved with their son Cyril to New York City. Here the artists took the wrapping idea one step further. The artists built sculptures that look like storefronts and draped them with fabric or brown wrapping paper, giving this everyday object an air of mystery and wonder.

The scale of the Christo and Jeanne-Claude's works continued to grow until they achieved epic proportions in 1968. The husband-wife team created what they called "temporary monuments."[33] Jeanne-Claude wrapped a three-story medieval tower and a baroque fountain in Spoleto, Italy, with woven polypropylene fabric and ropes. Meanwhile, Christo was working in Bern on the couple's first example of a fully wrapped building. He wrapped the Kunsthalle, a Swiss art museum, in clear polyethylene. A hole was cut through the plastic by the entrance

Gentle Disturbances

Artists Christo and Jeanne-Claude are famous for wrapping buildings and parks in plastic and canvas and creating what they call temporary monuments. In an interview posted on the Journal of Contemporary Art *Web site, the husband-wife team explain their concepts of space and art:*

Christo: Everything in the world is owned by somebody: somebody designed the sidewalks, or the streets, even the highway, somebody even designed the airways. 24 hours around the clock, we move in a highly precise space designed by politicians, urban planners, and of course that space is full of regulations, ownerships, jurisdictions, meanings. I love that space. We go in that space and we create gentle disturbances in that space. Basically, we are borrowing that space and use it intricately for a short time. . . . [One] of the most intimate projects that actually translates that is the one called "Wrapped Walkways" in Kansas City, Missouri, done in 1978. . . . The walkway was covered with saffron-colored fabric, very simple fabric. . . . [We] put one millimeter of folded fabric between your feet and the surface. . . . You never watch what you walk on, now, everybody was obliged to be aware of how he walked on that fabric, otherwise he would break his neck because there are many folds in the fabric. . . . [Suddenly] people were obliged to readjust themselves, to rethink how they moved through that space, think every path, think every step.

Jeanne-Claude: And maybe since the first time they watched their children take their first steps, they became conscious of their feet.

Quoted in Gianfranco Mantegna, "Christo and Jeanne-Claude," *Journal of Contemporary Art*. www.jca-online.com/christo.html.

so visitors could still enter the museum. In 1969, Christo and Jeanne-Claude wrapped the Museum of Contemporary Art in Chicago in a 10,000 square foot (900 sq. m.) greenish-brown tarpaulin held in place with 4,000 feet (1,219 m.) of Manila rope. Commenting on the project, art critic and journalist David Bourdon writes:

> If any building ever needed wrapping, it was Chicago's Museum of Contemporary Art, a banal, one story edifice . . . having about as much architectural charm as an old shoe box. . . . Christo and Jeanne-Claude considered the building perfect, because it looks like a package already, very anonymous. . . . Although they had just wrapped the Bern [Switzerland] Museum in translucent plastic, the Christos decided for aesthetic reasons to shroud the Chicago museum in greenish-brown tarpaulin, which would give greater physical presence to the building and make a better contrast with the

A view of the west façade of Christo and Jeanne-Claude's *Wrapped Reichstag, Project for Berlin, 1971–95.*

> snow. . . . The finished package had a stateliness and sobriety that considerably enhanced the building. In contrast to the Bern museum, with its veil of translucent plastic billowing like a loose summer garment, the Chicago museum was tightly swathed in heavy tarpaulins, as if bu.ndled against the city's blustery winter winds and snow.[34]

In 1969, Christo and Jeanne-Claude left the urban landscape and created *Wrapped Coast*, draping the rocky Australian coastline near Sydney with 1 million square feet (92,903.04 sq. m.) of woven erosion control fabric and polypropylene rope. Several years later, Christo and Jeanne-Claude added color to the environment around the Grand Hogback Mountain Range in Colorado. The work *Valley Curtain* spanned one side of Rifle Gap, a narrow valley, to the other with 142,000 square feet (13,192 sq. m.) of bright orange nylon fabric. The couple's next project, *Running Fence*, required 2,222,222 square feet (200,000 sq. m.) of white fabric fence 18 feet (5.5 m.) high. This fence ran across 24.5 miles (39.4 k.) of California landscape through Sonoma and Marin Counties to the Pacific Ocean.

These large projects brought both scorn and praise to the couple. However, the artists ignored critics and continued to imagine works of art on a grand scale. Each new project brought new difficulties that required long periods to solve. For example, in 1971 Christo and Jeanne-Claude first dreamed of wrapping the former German parliament building, the Reichstag. However, it took twenty-five years to come to fruition. During the two and a half decades of planning *Wrapped Reichstag* Christo and Jeanne-Claude attended countless zoning board hearings, public forums, parliamentary debates, public and private meetings, legal and contract negotiations, press conferences, materials' tests, and exhibitions. Hundreds of drawings and sketches were required as well as enormous effort and teamwork for the actual installations.

After the project was finally approved in 1994, the artists worked with ten German companies that employed manufacturers, iron workers, engineers, environmentalists, and construction workers. Finally in June 1995, Christo and Jeanne-Claude, accompanied by one hundred German mountain climbers, wrapped the Reichstag in 1,076,000 square feet (99,963.67 sq. m.) of thick woven, recyclable polypropylene fabric with an aluminum surface. The wrap was held in place by 51,181 feet (15,600 m.) of blue polypropylene rope.

Wrapped Reichstag was finished on June 24, 1995. More than 600,000 people came to view it the first day and a total of 5 million visitors came to view the work while it stood. The wrapping came off as scheduled, fourteen days later, after which all the materials were recycled.

As with all their projects, the artists refused to accept commercial sponsors. The total cost of *Wrapped Reichstag* was self-financed through sale of drawings, collages, scale models, and early works of the 1950s and 1960s. The *Wrapped Reichstag* had special significance for Christo. The Berlin Wall had fallen in 1989, and East and West Germany were reunited for the first time since World War II. Christo commented: "the artwork . . . expresses freedom, poetic freedom—all our projects are about freedom. This project cannot be bought or sold, nobody can charge, can sell tickets. Freedom is the enemy of possession. And possession is equal to permanence."[35]

"Drill a Hole in the Sky"

Christo's projects were executed on a grand scale that was unusual for most conceptual artists. Others created works that existed only as words printed on a page that were meant to evoke concepts in the minds of readers. For example, the 1964 book *Grapefruit; A Book of Instructions and Drawings* by Japanese-born artist Yoko Ono is filled with instructions. For *Hide and Seek Piece* Ono told readers, "Hide until everybody goes home. Hide until everybody forgets about you. Hide until everybody dies."[36]

Grapefruit was an extension of Ono's so-called instruction pieces. These were intended to free people's minds and allow them to focus on their own creativity rather than that of a professional artist. In the piece *Painting to Be Constructed in Your Head*, Ono instructed readers: "Go on transforming a square canvas in your head until it becomes a circle. Pick out any shape in the process and pin up or place on the canvas an object, a smell, a sound, or a color that came to mind in association with the shape." To create *Painting for the Skies*, readers were told, "Drill a hole in the sky. Cut out a paper the same size as the hole. Burn the paper. The sky should be pure blue."[37]

While much of Ono's work was whimsical, some of her pieces were inspired by horrors she witnessed as a child growing up in Japan during World War II. She was only twelve when Tokyo was firebombed by the United States and the cities of Hiroshima and Nagasaki were incinerated by nuclear

During the 1960s, artist Yoko Ono displayed artwork that conveyed both negative emotions about war as well as positive feelings that affirmed the power of imagination.

How to Share an Experience

In 1968 conceptual artist Yoko Ono spoke to Tony Elliot from Time Out *magazine. During the interview Ono explained that the objective of her art was not to shock people but to create unity and harmony in a warlike world:*

People think that I'm doing something shocking and ask me if I'm trying to shock people. The most shocking thing to me is that people have war, fight with each other and moreover take it for granted. The kind of thing I'm doing is almost too simple. I'm not interested in being unique or different. Everyone is different. . . . The problem is not how to become different or unique, but how to share an experience, how to be the same almost, how to communicate.

Basically I am interested in communication and therefore participation of everybody. I'm just part of the participation. . . . All my pieces are white because I think that white is the only color that allows imaginary color to be put on. In the Lisson Gallery I'm going to have a one room environment that's called "The Blue Room Event." The room is completely white and you're supposed to stay in the room until it becomes blue. . . . So what I'm trying to do is make something happen by throwing a pebble into the water and creating ripples. It's like starting a good motion. I don't want to control the ripples and everything.

Yoko Ono, "1968 Interview with Tony Elliot, *Time Out Magazine*," a-I-u.net. http://pers-www.wlv.ac.uk/%7Efa1871/yoko.html.

bombs. In her conceptual artwork, she tried to convey the loneliness of a child during war using art and performance.

One of Ono's most notorious works was based on her wartime experiences. In the 1966 performance *Cut Piece*, Ono dressed in a traditional Japanese kimono and sat motionless on a stage. She invited members of the audience to cut away pieces of cloth until, after about forty minutes, she was naked, her masklike face cold and unemotional. When explaining the meaning of *Cut Piece*, Ono said she wanted to express the isolation remembered from her childhood. She wanted the participants to "hear the kind of sounds that you hear in silence . . . to feel the environment and tension in people's vibrations . . . the sound of fear and darkness . . . [and] . . . alienation."[38]

Not all of Ono's work was so negative, however. She often used conceptual art as a way of evoking positive feelings and affirming the power of imagination. In 1966 Ono held a show, *Unfinished Paintings and Objects*, at the Indica Gallery in London. For this show the artist used found objects that were either transparent or painted white, shades meant to convey peace. For example, *White Chess Set* was a standard chess set, but since the board and all the pieces were white, the game, which symbolizes a battle, could not be played in the traditional manner.

John Lennon, a member of the Beatles rock group, attended this show and participated in one of the art pieces. He climbed a white ladder set in place to allow viewers to look at a piece of paper attached to the ceiling. Using a magnifying glass provided by Ono, Lennon read the tiny word "YES" written on the paper.

Other instruction pieces in the show encouraged visitor participation, a symbolic way of sharing the art with everyone. For example, *Painting to Hammer a Nail* consisted of a white panel, a hammer, and a jar of nails. A card instructed viewers to pound nails into the panel. *Add Color Painting* consisted of a wood panel and brushes and paints provided so patrons could add their own concepts to the work.

After Lennon attended *Unfinished Paintings and Objects*, he and Ono became inseparable. They were married in 1969 and Ono used Lennon's considerable fame and wealth to conduct a campaign for peace based on conceptual art. In December 1969, as the Vietnam War was raging, Lennon and Ono published the message, "WAR IS OVER! / IF YOU WANT IT / Happy Christmas from John & Yoko."[39] This message was placed on billboards (with appropriate translations) in Hong Kong, London, Tokyo, New York City, and other cities throughout the world. It was also included in the Lennon song "Happy Xmas (War Is Over)" and distributed on posters, postcards, handbills, newspaper advertisements, and radio ads.

A Cog in the Machine

Ono and Christo were among the few conceptualists who were able to speak to a wide audience. Most other conceptual artists rejected the art market, declined to create art objects to sell, and labored in obscurity. This made it difficult for the conceptual art movement to hold together.

Although the movement peaked in popularity in the 1960s and 1970s, it has had a lasting impact on art. Artists working in other postmodern styles, such as installation art and appropriation art, incorporate conceptual ideas into their work through the use of words and language in their pieces. In doing so, the artists provide instructions or notions that help the viewer understand, interpret, or add to the work. In this way, the concept remains an important cog in the machine that makes the art.

Installation Art

In 1803 German Romantic painter Philipp Otto Runge created stunning visions on canvases filled with cherubs, angels, clouds, oceans, and flowers. Runge hoped to evoke mystical experiences in the viewer, and to further that idea the painter invented something he called total art. For his total art exhibitions, Runge envisioned exhibiting his paintings surrounded by elaborately sculpted frames and living plants in a specially designed gallery. As visitors entered the exhibition they would be greeted by an orator reading poetry and an orchestra playing specially composed music.

In Runge's day total art exhibitions were unheard of and there were strict divisions between art exhibits, literary readings, and musical concerts. However, about forty years after Runge's death in 1810, German composer Richard Wagner wrote a two-hundred-page essay called "The Art-Work of the Future," in which he proposed creating a total artwork, called *Gesamtkunstwerk*, or "fusion of the arts." This concept would produce a unification of music, song, dance, poetry, visual arts, and stagecraft.

By the late 1960s the concept of total art had taken on a new name: installation art. In the decades since, installation art exhibits, featuring painting, sculpture, words, found objects, photos, music, videos, and digital media, have been regular features at museums, galleries, and other art spaces.

Time and Space

Runge hoped to create a calming experience for patrons by blending his total art exhibition into a seamless, harmonious, and spiritually uplifting display. The goal of the installation artist is generally the opposite. Postmodern artists often load gallery spaces with dissimilar, unrelated, and obscure items. Rather than create harmony, these combinations of painting,

Although he was not the first to propose total art, around 1850 German composer Richard Wagner wrote a two-hundred page essay titled "The Art-Work of the Future," in which he suggested a "fusion of the arts."

sculpture, poem, prose, and nonart materials are meant to evoke complex emotions such as puzzlement, longing, wistfulness, sadness, elation, or even anger.

As in conceptual art, the concept or idea of the installation might be more important than the actual materials that make up the exhibit. While the viewer might react to the art in a certain way, he or she might not understand what the artist is trying to say. Museum curator Mark Rosenthal explains in *Understanding Installation Art*: "The [goal] of the modern installation artist . . . [is] how to reflect the experience of life—its complex issues, aspects, and appearances. The technique of installation has proved to be a useful tool by which to . . . speak about and investigate life."[40]

Like conceptual artists, installation artists also attempt to redefine art, the artist, exhibition space, and the art market. Traditionally, paintings have been lavishly framed and isolated on gallery walls while sculptures were displayed upon pedestals. Patrons stood behind velvet ropes or lines drawn on the floor so as not to intrude upon the seemingly sacred space surrounding the artwork. Installation artists do away with those concepts.

Patrons visiting an installation enter a room or space that is a surrounding artistic environment of sights, sounds, and even smells. They wander between different aspects of this environment, sometimes walking upon it, kicking it, or rearranging it. Computers, boom boxes, and video players invite viewers to push buttons, dance, or otherwise participate in the artistic space created by the installation. As Rosenthal writes, "[The] viewer is . . . swept up in a work of art much larger in expanse than an individual object can normally create. . . . [The] artist has created an arrangement that is an integrated, cohesive, carefully contrived whole."[41]

Installation art is different from traditional art in that it takes place in time and space. A conventional painting or sculpture freezes a moment in time—and might be understood with only a few moments' study. The installation space, on the other hand, may occupy a viewer's attention for many minutes or even hours. Rosenthal compares the time and space aspects of an installation to life itself: "The viewer is asked to investigate the work of art much as he or she might explore some phenomenon in life, making one's way through actual space and time in order to gain knowledge. Just as life consists of one perception followed by another, each a fleeting . . . moment, an installation courts the same dense, [momentary] experience."[42]

Environments and Happenings

The postmodern roots of installation art may be traced to the late 1950s when American painter, performer, and conceptual artist Allan Kaprow invented what he called "Environments." Kaprow considered New York's high-priced galleries, filled with sterile white walls, barren and uninspiring. These were places for "looking not touching."[43] He wished to make art in places that were "organic, fertile, and even dirty."[44] Therefore, Kaprow chose empty lots, dirty lofts, closed shops, abandoned buildings, and church basements to create his environments.

Kaprow's first event, "18 Happenings in 6 Parts," took place in 1959 in three rooms of the Reuben Gallery that had been outfitted with clear plastic walls. An orchestra played with toy instruments while photographic slides were projected on one wall. Performers walked through the rooms reading from books or moving their arms at odd angles choreographed like dance moves. Meanwhile, an artist painted a canvas, pausing to light matches while a woman stood nearby squeezing an orange. Visitors were given tickets that directed them to sit in specific rooms for a particular length of time then move on to another aspect of the installation.

Pop artists Robert Rauschenberg and Jasper Johns participated in the event, which helped Kaprow get good reviews from the art press. In the years that followed, Kaprow's events were eagerly sought out by New York's trendiest art followers but were often difficult to find since they were staged in odd, out-of-the-way places.

Artist Allan Kaprow is credited with developing the roots of installation art in the late 1950s. He traded in traditional art galleries for empty lots, abandoned buildings, and church basements to create what he called his "environments."

KAPROW'S *Words*

In 1962 Allan Kaprow held a happening called Words *at a New York gallery. The event is described by Jeff Kelly in* Childsplay: The Art of Allan Kaprow:

Kaprow divided the gallery space, which was inside an apartment, into two rooms. [In the] first, outer room . . . hundreds of strips of paper, each containing a single hand-written word, were stapled onto the other two walls; here, visitors were encouraged to tear off the strips and replace them with others that had been nailed to a central post. All the words on cloth and paper had been randomly gathered from "poetry books, newspapers, comic magazines, the telephone book, popular love stories," and so forth.

Crudely lettered overhead signs urged visitors to "staple word strips," "play," "tear off new words from post and staple them up," and "make new poems," among other actions. . . . Another sign, "lissen here hear records," directed visitors to three record players, on which recordings of lectures, shouts, advertisements, nonsensical ramblings, and so forth could be played simultaneously.

The smaller, inner room, maybe eight feet square, was painted blue and illuminated by a lone light bulb. Overhead was a black plastic sheet, creating a false ceiling that made the dark room seem like a graffiti space, recalling alleys and public toilets. . . . Hanging from slits in the plastic ceiling were torn strips of cloth, and clipped onto these were many small pieces of paper with handwritten notes. Near the entrance, paper, clips, and pencils were provided for visitors to add their own notes.

Jeff Kelly, *Childsplay: The Art of Allan Kaprow*. Berkeley and Los Angeles: University of California Press, 2004, p. 71.

Kaprow's "18 Happenings in 6 Parts" helped coin the now-famous term "happening." Although the artist originally used it to indicate a rehearsed, strictly choreographed production, the word has come to mean a spontaneous undirected event. While this was not Kaprow's original intent, his later happenings did become less structured.

For example, in the 1960 happening "Apple Shrine," Kaprow filled a long narrow room in a church basement with a maze of chicken wire, colored lights, bunched-up newspaper, straw, cloth, fake and real apples, and piles of garbage. This created an unpleasantly closed in, or claustrophobic, atmosphere, which smelled, oddly, of the fresh apples which were strewn about on the floor and kicked and crushed by visitors. Kaprow stated that he created the piece to draw attention to everyday environments generally ignored by people who live in them:

> [We] must become preoccupied with and even dazzled by the space and objects of our everyday life, either our bodies, clothes, rooms, or, if need be, the vastness of Forty-second Street. . . . [We] shall utilize the specific substances of sight, sound, movement, people, odors, touch. Objects of every sort are materials for the new art: paint, chairs, food, electric and neon lights, smoke, water, old socks, a dog, movies, a thousand other things.[45]

Kaprow also wished to create tension, risk, excitement, and even fear during his happenings. For his next event, "A Spring Happening" in 1961, he threatened the audience with a large power mower and electric fan in a dark tunnel.

In September 1962 Kaprow's *Words* pioneered the post-modern concept of incorporating words and language into an art piece. For the event the artist filled two small gallery rooms with hundreds of strips of paper containing random words. Visitors were encouraged to rearrange the words into sentences, poems, or nonsensical phrases, or add their own words to the displays. This happening was meant to draw attention to ways in which words assault the senses in an urban environment. As Kaprow explained:

> I am involved with the city atmosphere of billboards, newspapers, scrawled pavements and alley walls, in the drone of a lecture, whispered secrets, pitchmen in Times Square, fun-parlors, bits of stories in conversations overheard at the Automat [restaurant]. All this has been compressed and shaped into a situation which, in order to "live" in the fullest sense . . . [the artist must] bring words to life.[46]

By the mid-1960s Kaprow abandoned his concept of happenings because the word had been adopted by mass culture. As he told an interviewer in 1988: "Political uprisings on campuses and advertisements for butter and brassieres were all using the word [happenings] . . . in ways that had nothing to do with my original sense. It became so foreign to me I just dropped it."[47]

Womanhouse

Kaprow went back to painting in the 1970s, but his influential happenings had a lasting impact on the postmodern world. One of his main points—that the world could be seen from different, nontraditional perspectives—was particularly resonant to female artists. Many were part of the burgeoning women's liberation movement and had formed art collectives where they could discuss the discrimination against women artists in the male-dominated art world.

In 1970 one of the first New York collectives, Women Artists in Revolution (WAR), not only provided support for women but organized demonstrations for equality. For example, in 1971 WAR protested the annual exhibition at the Whitney Museum of American Art because only 8 of the 143 painters displayed there were women. The Whitney responded by increasing women's participation to 22 percent the following year. In the years that followed, "Feminism . . . [became] the most powerful . . . political force in the art world,"[48] according to art history professor Irving Sandler in *Art of the Postmodern Era.*

In 1970 California feminist Judy Chicago created the first college-level feminist art course at Fresno State College. Two years later, Chicago, Miriam Schapiro, and twenty-two stu-

Feminist artist Judy Chicago addresses the audience at the opening of the Elizabeth A. Sackler Center for Feminist Art at the Brooklyn Museum. Chicago created the first feminist art course of its kind at Fresno State College in 1970.

dents from the Fresno class created a major installation called *Womanhouse*. The artists took over an abandoned mansion in Hollywood and converted it to an installation. According to Schapiro, the exhibit was based on the "age-old female activity of homemaking. . . . Womanhouse became a repository of the daydreams women have as they wash, bake, cook, sew, clean, and iron their lives away. The environment became a kind of *Gesamtkunstwerk* of women's images."[49]

Working with materials such as shower caps, nightgowns, women's underwear, laundry, and other typically feminine items, women transformed the cold, decrepit mansion. The rooms included Beth Bachenheimer's *Shoe Closet*, Judy Chicago's *Menstruation Bathroom*, Sherry Brody's *Lingerie Pillows*, Brody and Schapiro's *Doll House*, and Faith Wilding's *Womb Room*. The installation *Linen Closet* by Sandra Orgel is described by Carrie Mae Weems on the Womanhouse Web page: "*Linen Closet* . . . shows a women trapped inside a linen closet with neatly folded towels and her head in what appears almost like a guillotine. One leg is outside as if she is free but not free from the female experience we are taught to embrace and feel stuck inside."[50]

In addition to art, the exhibit featured performances by the artists, which were documented in the film *Womanhouse* by Johanna Demetrakas.

The Dinner Party

Chicago's next collaborative installation project celebrated the accomplishments of women rather than the oppression many felt. Produced between 1973 and 1979, *The Dinner Party* is a huge banquet table in the shape of an equilateral triangular 48 feet (14.6m) on each side. There are thirty-nine place settings on the table, each one representing a famous woman. The three sides of the table represent different periods in history. Wing I contains thirteen place settings for women "From Prehistory to the Roman Empire," including the Primordial Goddess, the firstborn deity from Greek myth; Ishtar, the Assyrian goddess of fertility; and Hypatia, an Egyptian mathematical scholar killed by a religious mob.

Wing II is dedicated to thirteen women "From the Beginnings of Christianity to the Reformation." This side includes Saint Bridget, a mystic, saint, and founder of the Bridgettine Order; Eleanor of Aquitaine, one of the wealthiest and most powerful women in Europe during the Middle Ages; and Elizabeth I, Queen of England and Ireland from 1558 to 1603.

Wing III of *The Dinner Party* is devoted to women "From the American to the Women's Revolution." This side has place settings for Sacagawea, a Shoshone woman who accompanied Lewis and Clark in their exploration of the western United States; Sojourner Truth, an African American abolitionist and women's rights activist; and Georgia O'Keeffe, an artist who mixed realism and abstraction in her paintings of nature. The entire installation sits on what is called the Heritage Floor, with 999 names of other famous women inscribed upon it.

Judy Chicago's piece titled *The Dinner Party* is a celebration of women's history and accomplishments from prehistoric times through the twentieth century.

The Dinner Party was assembled by hundreds of volunteers, and each individual place setting contains an elaborately shaped ceramic or painted china plate, a needlework runner, a ceramic chalice, and a knife, fork, and spoon. Each plate and runner is custom-made for the individual it represents. Sojourner Truth's setting is described on the Brooklyn Museum Web site:

> [The setting] combines references to her African heritage as well as her prominent roots in American history. In this runner, Chicago connects the African origins of quilting with its history in the United States. The edging of the runner is an African strip-weave technique, traditionally used by slaves, combined with a piece-working technique imported to the United States by European women. . . . Sojourner Truth's plate . . . shows three faces, one turned to the left, one facing straight ahead, and one turned to the right. The faces, which evoke African masks, share a single female body, suggested by the rounded breasts.[51]

The Dinner Party was first exhibited at the San Francisco Museum of Modern Art on March 14, 1979, where approximately 100,000 people came to see it during the three-month display. After its premiere, *The Dinner Party* went on a nine-year international tour across the United States, Canada, Scotland, England, Germany, and Australia and was viewed by over a million people. In 2007 *The Dinner Party* was permanently installed in the Elizabeth A. Sackler Center for Feminist Art in the Brooklyn Museum in New York.

A Space Before Language

The huge public interest in *The Dinner Party* proved that installation art was a valuable commodity for galleries and museums. Although the genre was founded as a reaction against commercialism, since the 1980s installations have drawn large crowds to most major exhibitions. As Bishop writes, exhibitors "came to rely increasingly on installation art as a way to create memorable, high-impact gestures within large exhibition spaces. . . . Installation art . . . is capable of creating grand

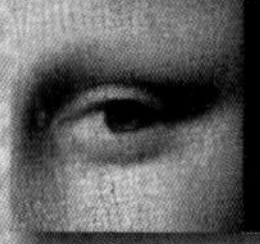

Activating the Body Experience

The installation work of Ann Hamilton is known for its ability to stimulate the senses of the viewer. The "Understanding Installation Art" Web page describes Hamilton's 1999 piece Myein:

Ann Hamilton, who was chosen to install a work in [Italy's] neo-classical pavilion in Venice . . . placed an enormous veil of water glasses in front of the pavilion that both framed and radically obscured the structure's 90-foot length and 18-foot height. Set three yards from the entrance, the steel-and-glass wall distorted the pavilion, making it look something like the other side of a fun-house mirror. Inside, she had some fuchsia-hued powder cascading slowly down the walls. This garish powder piled up on Braille dots Hamilton arranged that spelled out verses relating to human suffering. The powder slowly descended from the top of the gallery walls, and as time passed, the powder built up around the white dots, making them partially visible, yet still frustrating the viewer's ability to read what they say. Muttering softly in the background was Hamilton's whispered rendition of excerpts from Abraham Lincoln's second inaugural address, which deals with curing the wounds caused by slavery. . . . Katy Kline, the director of the Bowdoin College Museum of Art in Maine, who chose the work, says, "She invites the viewer into a set of visible and auditory conditions where their entire bodily experience is activated. They are swept into a state of awareness beyond that of the normal viewer."

Dummies.com, "Understanding Installation Art." www.dummies.com/WileyCDA/DummiesArticle/id-1139.html.

visual impact by addressing the whole space and generating striking photographic opportunities."[52]

Like the spaces where they were exhibited, some art installations grew to gigantic proportions. In the early 1990s Ohio-born artist Ann Hamilton became known for using large quantities of unusual materials to create installations in vast spaces. For the 1991 Spoleto Festival in Charleston, South Carolina, Hamilton created *indigo blue* by artfully arranging 14,000 pounds (6,350kg) of used blue cotton work clothes in an abandoned auto dealer garage. Indigo is a plant traditionally used to make blue dye, and the piece was conceived as a tribute to the millions of "blue collar" workers, or factory workers, who have contributed so much to American prosperity. The empty clothing is symbolic of those workers whose names and deeds are forgotten by history.

Hamilton's subsequent projects were meant to invoke thoughts of livestock commonly used for commodities or killed for food. To have maximum impact, the artist created the installations to upset the patron's sense of balance, sight, hearing, and smell. For *between taxonomy and communion* Hamilton laid sheep fleeces upon the floor and covered them with sheets of glass that cracked when viewers walked over them. In *tropos* the artist filled a 5,000-square-foot factory space (464 sq. m) with horsehair colored from black to blonde, sewn in bundles. The uneven floor space created by the hair, taken from slaughtered horses, was difficult to walk through and filled the room with a pungent smell. In the center of the room, the artist sat alone at a metal desk, burning printed text in a book, line by line, using an engraving tool.

From the perimeter of the room, located outside the windows, patrons heard the murmur of a man struggling to speak in a garbled language. The slow speech had the effect of transforming the empty warehouse into an otherworldly, mental space. The meaning of the piece is explained on the PBS Web site *Art:21*: "While the large quantity of horsehair is at once overpowering, horsehair as a material bridges the gap between animal and human, having been used by wigmakers for centuries. What Hamilton carves out of this warehouse is a space before language, where dyslexic speech calls out from behind frosted windows and where the gap between horse and humanity is bridged by a material which also serves to distinguish the two from each other: the written word."[53]

Darkness and Light

Hamilton uses natural and found materials to manipulate the viewer's sensory experiences. Other installation artists use contrasts between dark and light to disorient and control the behavior of the public. To do so, the artists build environments that require patrons to walk through twisting, turning, darkened or pitch-black corridors that block out the typically bright white light of the museum. Such passageways often lead to installations where video monitors, lights, and mirrors greet the disoriented patrons. Bishop comments on this type of experience:

> As we fumble for the reassuring presence of a wall to orient us, the blackness seems to press against our eyes. Even when the light of a video projection becomes visible as the main focus of the work, we still strain to locate our body in relation to the dark environment. . . . [These] dark installations suggest our dissolution; they seem to dislodge or annihilate our sense of self.[54]

Los Angeles–born artist James Turrell is widely known for his installations, which enclose viewers in order to control their perception of light. In many of Turrell's installations, patrons must walk through disorienting pitch-black corridors that lead to larger darkened rooms where the artist masterfully manipulates the visual senses through optical illusions. For example, when viewers enter the installation *Atlan* at the Art Tower Mito in Japan, they see what appears to be a deep blue painting on the far wall. As eyes adjust to the darkness, the blue seems to swell and change color. Often, when viewers walk toward the blue for closer inspection, they reach out to touch what appears to be a solid glowing panel. They are then startled to find that the large rectangle is actually an open window into another empty, light-filled room. The eyes continue to play tricks. Although the opposite wall of the blue room appears close, when viewers reach through the window to touch it they find it is far away. According to *Art:21*: "This window in the wall is like a portal onto another world, providing a view of a limitless space like the ocean or a starless sky. The work's infinite view is ultimately the product of one's own sense perceptions, and the viewer becomes aware of his or her own beliefs and habits of looking."[55]

The Ganzfeld Effect

Turrell has created installations similar to *Atlan* with red, pink, green, beige, and gray rooms. These light installations create a visual phenomenon known as the Ganzfeld effect. This disorienting effect occurs when the brain registers depth, color, surface, and brightness as a single sensation. The Ganzfeld effect creates a sort of blindness comparable to an arctic whiteout in which victims cannot tell up from down.

When a Turrell installation creates the Ganzfeld effect, patrons are ensnared in a space where the walls, floor, and ceiling seem to be blurred or absent. This upsets their sense of balance. Bishop describes how Turrell's installation *Arhirit* affected patrons at the Whitney:

> Turrell could not fully have anticipated the physical response elicited by this installation; without form for the eye to latch onto, visitors fell over, disoriented, and were unable to keep their balance; many had to crawl through the exhibition on their hands and knees in order to prevent themselves from being "lost in the light." . . . [Several visitors] brought lawsuits against Turrell after having fallen through what they perceived to be a solid wall, but which in fact was just the edge of a Ganzfeld.[56]

Questioning Reality

Turrell's manipulation of space and light creates illusions that could never be evoked by traditional painting and sculpture. As with most postmodernist installations, the environment is redefined in ways that force viewers to question or doubt

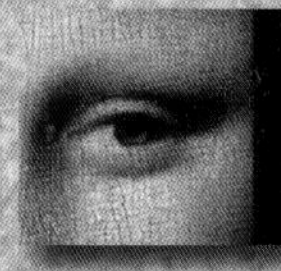

Video Installation

Installation artists have used moving images in their pieces from the time primitive video cameras were developed in the early 1970s. Since that time, video installations have improved with technology to include the latest advancements, including plasma screens, video projectors, and computers. Bill Viola is a seminal artist who shaped video installation art. His 1991 piece The Stopping Mind *was notable for its use of video and sound, as Claire Bishop explains in* Installation Art:

The four-screen installation . . . offers a dark, protean [varied] rush of images (operations, barking dogs, owls flying, desert at night, figures tossing in their sleep) in a way that only just keeps disintegration below the surface. The camerawork is not slick and polished, but harnesses the glitches and errors inherent in video technology to exaggerate its affective impact. The staging of these screens reinforces this fragmentation further, entering into a black chamber, you encounter the four hanging screens, each showing frozen imagery. Moving towards the center you hear a man whispering a description, at high speed, of his body's progressive loss of sensation in an unknown black space. A loud grating noise suddenly sets the images on the screens into motion and we are harried by jolting camerawork. The shock of this movement catches us off-guard. Just as suddenly, the screens become still and silent, and the whispered voice resumes its description of sinking down into blackness.

Claire Bishop, *Installation Art*. New York: Routledge, 2005, p. 97.

Artist Bill Viola has been recognized for shaping video installation art and is famous for his 1991 piece The Stopping Mind.

conventional wisdom. It is little wonder then that installations by Turrell, Hamilton, Chicago, and others are popular. For the price of admission, gallery goers can enter a temporary world with its own unique concepts of light, space, time, history, up, and down. In such places the mundane, the normal, and even the concept of reality vanishes. What is left is a sense of liberation that cannot be felt by simply gazing at an oil painting hung on a wall at a museum.

4

Appropriation Art

Renowned folksinger Pete Seeger once jokingly said, "Plagiarism is basic to all culture."[57] Seeger did not mean that taking credit for another person's ideas or words advances society. He meant that culture is often remade by those who take other peoples' ideas, words, art, or songs, alter them, and transmit them in a new way. This is the basic idea behind sampling, the act of taking a portion, or sample, of one sound recording and reusing it as an element of a new recording.

In the world of postmodern art, the act of borrowing one creation and using it in a new way is called appropriation. The most famous early example of appropriation art is Marcel Duchamp's 1917 *Fountain*. Although the urinal was made by the Bedfordshire company, when Duchamp appropriated it, signed it, and displayed it as art, he started a trend that continues to this day.

"A Tissue of Quotations"

Pop artists such as Andy Warhol were famous for appropriating commercial images for their creations, but the term "appropriation art" did not come into common use until the early 1980s. At that time, Pennsylvania-born artist Sherrie Levine

A typical Walker Evans photograph depicting a poor family on their porch during the Great Depression. In 1981 artist Sherrie Levine rephotographed much of Evans's work and displayed it as her own in a concept that has become known as appropriation art.

created controversy by directly appropriating pictures taken by famed photographer Walker Evans. The Evans photographs depicted poor white Alabama sharecroppers living in squalor during the Great Depression in the mid-1930s. They were originally published in the best-selling book *Let Us Now Praise Famous Men*, a book that brought attention to rural poverty and the need for welfare programs in the 1940s.

Levine rephotographed the photos directly from an Evans exhibition catalog. In 1981 she displayed them as her own work, without making any changes, at the Metro Pictures gallery in New York at a show called "After Walker Evans." In true postmodernist fashion, Levine's concept became more important than the photos or the images displayed.

In her artistic statement for "After Walker Evans," Levine claimed that all images created by photographers or painters

A One-Liner Art Prank

In the early 1980s Sherrie Levine rephotographed pictures taken by famed photographer Walker Evans and displayed them in a show called After Walker Evans. *By appropriating the photographs, Levine gave them a new meaning. In 2001 Michael Mandiberg scanned these same photographs and created the Web site AfterSherrieLevine.com. According to Mandiberg, the site is meant "as a comment on how we come to know information in this burgeoning digital age." Mandiberg further explains the inspiration behind AfterSherrieLevine.com:*

A lot of conceptual art is an inside joke, and a lot of these jokes are one-liners. This site (like Sherrie Levine's work itself) is no different. Conceptual art positions itself within cultural theory and art history in order to "make a point" yet this point is often esoteric, inaccessible, and without real philosophical depth. In part, AfterSherrieLevine.com is this one-liner art prank. . . . I scanned these same photographs out of the same book [Sherrie did], and created this web site to facilitate their dissemination. I have done this both as a critique, and as a collaboration, to use her own phrase. By scanning these images, I am bringing her critique into the digital age: one is increasingly likely to see (Walker Evans') images on a computer screen, and not in a text book; similarly the tools of image production have shifted to digital media. By distributing these images for free, like open source software . . . I have taken a strong step towards creating an art object that has cultural value, but little or no economic value.

Michael Mandiberg, "AfterSherrieLevine.com," 2001. www.AfterSherrieLevine.com/index.html.

are plagiarized. For example, da Vinci did not create the woman portrayed in *Mona Lisa*, he only copied, or appropriated, her image and immortalized it with paint. In the same way, Walker Evans simply captured with a camera the faces and bodies of his subjects and the objects they place around them in their homes. Levine commented on this concept: "We know that a picture is but a space in which a variety of images, none of them original, blend and clash. A picture is a tissue of quotations [thoughts expressed by others] drawn from innumerable centers of culture. . . . We can only imitate a gesture that is never original."[58] By challenging the concept of originality, Levine also protested the idea of art as a product to be bought and sold. Other postmodern concepts concerning the exhibit are explored on the MOMA Web site: "The series, entitled After Walker Evans, became a landmark of postmodernism . . . and an elegy [funeral dirge] on the death of modernism. Far from a high-concept cheap shot, Levine's works from this series tell the story of our perpetually dashed hopes to create meaning, the inability to recapture the past, and our own lost illusions."[59]

"A Deceptively Simple Act"

Like Levine, Richard Prince got his start rephotographing the work of others. But instead of appropriating famous art photographs, Prince took possession of advertising images created to sell cigarettes, expensive watches, perfumes, and designer clothing. Prince did not often photograph the entire ad. Rather, his images capture a fragment of the original photo, giving the appropriated picture a new meaning. For example, the 1989 *Untitled (cowboy)* is a photo of a cowboy riding a galloping horse with a lasso in his hand. Taken from a Marlboro cigarette ad, the cowboy in the lower right corner of the photograph is surrounded by blurred clouds and sky.

Untitled (cowboy) is from Prince's best-known series of images, all of which were appropriated from Marlboro ads. The photos were meant to explore the idea of the cowboy as an example of the rugged individual who represented the ideal American male. However, since such a man only existed in

Heroic Images of Cowboys

In 2003 writer and curator Mia Fineman wrote an article in Slate *about Richard Prince and the artistic success he found by rephotographing cigarette ads:*

In 1983, [Prince] showed a group of photographs called "Cowboys," in which he re-photographed Marlboro cigarette ads, cropping out the text and blowing them up to nearly life-size. These heroic images of Madison Avenue cowboys perfectly embodied the screwy zeitgeist [spirit of the times] of the Reagan years: a B-movie cowboy for president and a pill-popping first lady whose political mantra was "Just Say No." The "Cowboy" . . . appropriations were like projections from inside the vaults of the cultural unconscious.

Around this time, academic critics like Hal Foster championed Prince's work as part of a postmodern critique of commodity culture and as a definitive break with the fusty [stale] traditions of high modernism. Prince's deadpan, re-photographed pictures were seen as harbingers [forerunners] of "the death of painting"—or at least as a challenge to the cherished notions of authenticity that painting stood for. A few years later, some of these critics ate their words when they found that the strategy of appropriation had lost its critical teeth. Displayed in the homes of wealthy collectors, the pictures of cowboys that once advertised Marlboro cigarettes had now become high-end advertisements for a new brand-name in the cultural marketplace: Richard Prince.

Mia Fineman, "The Pleasure Principle: Richard Prince's Post-Pulp Art Takes a New Step," *Slate*, October 30, 2003. www.slate.com/id/2090475.

the fantasy worlds of ads and movies, Prince believed he could only be possessed through artificial creations: "The pictures I went after; STOLE, were too good to be true. They were about wishful thinking, secret desires and dreams, not only the public's but [my] own."[60]

Prince not only appropriated single images but in the mid-1980s began to use what were called "gang formats," or multiple images on one page. Inspired by the word gang, Prince stole images associated with large groups, or gangs. These included photos of drag racers, heavy metal bands, surfers, and the stereotypical Hell's Angels bikers and their women. Commenting on these photos, taken from ads and magazine articles, Prince stated that he identified not only with "teen delinquency and anti-social behavior—but a lot of people living on their own terms."[61]

Prince has been sued by the creators of original images and criticized for stealing the work of others. However, in 2005 *Untitled (cowboy)* sold for more than $1.2 million, setting a record for the most expensive photo ever sold at auction. Describing Price's impact on postmodern art, the Guggenheim Museum Web page states:

> His deceptively simple act . . . of rephotographing advertising images and presenting them as his own ushered in an entirely new, critical approach to art-making—one that questioned notions of originality and the privileged status of the unique aesthetic object. Prince's technique involves appropriation; he pilfers freely from the vast image bank of popular culture to create works that simultaneously embrace and critique a quintessentially American sensibility. . . . [And his art] registers prevalent themes in our social landscape, including a fascination with rebellion, an obsession with fame, and a preoccupation with the tawdry and the illicit.[62]

Your Body Is a Battleground

Prince appropriations were not presented with specific messages. Viewers could look at his Marlboro man and see him as

Artist Barbara Kruger's 1990 piece titled *I Shop Therefore I Am* has ironically been reproduced on items like shopping bags, billboards, and T-shirts and shows how consumerism and art can be intermingled.

an American hero, an ironic stereotype, or simply a model in a cigarette ad. However, in the 1980s many appropriation artists used less subtle means to make philosophical and political points. For example, New Jersey–born artist Barbara Kruger gained recognition by appropriating black-and-white photographs from magazines, cropping out a portion of the image, and crudely enlarging it to a massive size. The artist then layered messages over the photos printed in bold white lettering highlighted in bright red text boxes.

Many of Kruger's themes focus on the politics of gender, race, sexuality, consumerism, and cultural stereotypes. While using simple short phrases, her messages have a visual punch because they are juxtaposed, or put side by side with, the contrasting images of the advertising photos. For example, in *Your Body Is a Battleground*, Kruger pictured a female model's face with the words "Your body" pasted across the top of the photo, "is a" in the center, and "battleground" across the bottom. The left half of the photo is a regular black-and-white picture, while the right half is a photo negative where the light and dark parts of the image are reversed. This 1989 work became famous after it was used on posters advertising a major pro-choice march in Washington, D.C.

Another famous Kruger piece, the 1990 *I Shop Therefore I Am*, is described by Monica Racic in *d/visible* magazine.

> The title of the piece, of course in white Futura lettering, is written in a red rectangle and held between the thumb and middle finger as though it were a credit card or some sort or identification. A clear reference to [French philosopher René] Descartes "I think therefore I am," Kruger jokingly implies that in our society consumerism is valued and elevated to a level so high it supersedes consciousness. But on some levels could this be more than a joke? After all, a joke is usually half of the truth. Just think of the numbing effects advertising can have. There is more than humor in Kruger's piece. Although, the fact that the design was featured on a shopping bag is quite entertaining, particularly for the person who sees someone else carrying it.[63]

Perhaps as humorous, or ironic, Kruger's messages have been reproduced as typical advertising on matchbooks, billboards, T-shirts, television ads, and in subway cars. They have also been exhibited in museums and public spaces around the world. By contrasting beauty, tragedy, humor, and politics, Kruger's work cuts through viewers' defenses and makes them take notice. Commenting on this technique, artist and activist Avram Finkelstein states:

> Some of it has to do with putting political information into environments where people are unaccustomed to finding it. It's confrontational . . . and creates a whole other context—a whole other environment. People are less defensive. It's very different from being handed a leaflet where you automatically know someone's trying

to tell you something. . . . So it's an appropriation tactic that's somewhat confrontational and has been very effective.[64]

Images in Front of Everybody

While Kruger and Prince rephotographed advertisements, in the late 1990s painter Damien Loeb skillfully used paint and brush to appropriate photographic images. These were recreated from found images pirated from art, newspaper clippings, fashion, and advertising. In 1998 Loeb produced controversy with *Sunlight Mildness.* The realistic painting shows four teenagers cruising in a convertible, an image directly appropriated from the photograph *Mijanou and Friends* by Lauren Greenfield. Loeb painted this image in the foreground of the work and juxtaposed it with a background image of a white policeman shooting at a group of black people. Although the meaning of Greenfield's image was completely changed by the imagery in the background, she successfully sued Loeb and settled out of court for an undisclosed amount. Loeb offers his explanation about the controversy: "The matter is simple for me. The images I saw were in front of everybody and so I commented on them."[65]

Although Loeb claims the settlement nearly bankrupted him, he continued to appropriate images for his work. Moving into the sphere of common cultural images, Loeb began creating paintings from movie stills he captured off DVDs. According to Richard Klein, director of exhibitions from the Aldrich Contemporary Art Museum in Connecticut:

> The second phase of Loeb's work was based in the artist's obsession with the craftsmanship of Hollywood, coupled with his ability to carefully analyze and

Painter Damien Loeb (pictured here) believes that he has the right to appropriate images for his artwork even though he has been successfully sued for using these images.

> dissect film that came about with the introduction of the DVD. Loeb has an archive of films on DVD, which . . . he utilized for a series of paintings based primarily on panning or tracking shots from horror and sci-fi films such as *The Shining* and *Close Encounters*. Loeb would freeze individual frames that comprise a lengthy shot, and subsequently fuse them together using both Photoshop [graphics editing software] and traditional collage techniques, creating images that don't exist in the original film.[66]

In recent years Loeb has moved away from image appropriation. His latest work features paintings of his own digital photographs that he has manipulated in a computer. Whatever the source, Loeb's images, which have been called photorealism, or hyperrealism, provide a view of manipulated reality that is both otherworldly and down-to-earth.

"Feel Good Paintings For Feel Bad Times"

Loeb's idea of lifting images from movies and ads was first popularized by Andy Warhol in the 1960s. Three decades later, New York–based artist Deborah Kass pirated Warhol's pop art style, bringing the concept full circle.

Warhol's art was created in his large New York studio called the Factory. The Factory employed silk-screeners to churn out portraits of the rich and famous, including actress Marilyn Monroe, former first lady Jackie Kennedy, and Chinese dictator Mao Zedong. The silk screen process involves burning a photographic image onto a framed screen. Ink or paint is poured into the screen and transferred to canvas, cloth, or paper with a squeegee. This process allowed Warhol's workers to make an infinite number of prints or put several of the exact same images on one piece of canvas using garish pinks, reds, greens, and yellows.

In 1992 Kass appropriated Warhol's silk screen style to explore her identity as a Jewish lesbian. Whereas Warhol

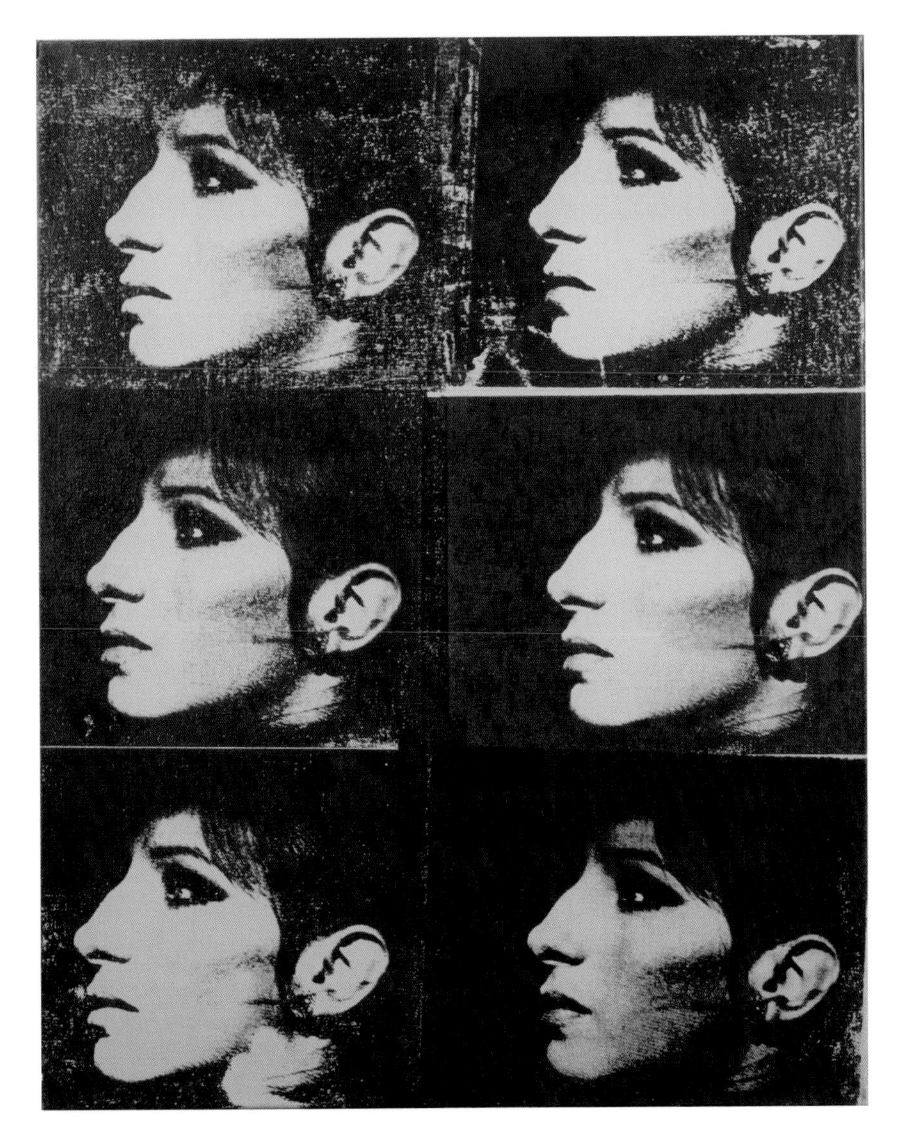

Artist Deborah Kass's *Six Blue Barbras* painted in 1992 and part of Kass's *The Jewish Jackie* series appropriated Andy Warhol's silk screen style that he made famous during the 1960s.

silk-screened images of rock singer Elvis Presley, Kass created the *My Elvis* series. This consisted of multiple images of singer and actress Barbra Streisand dressed like a young man in the movie *Yentl*. Where Warhol screened Chairman Mao, Kass portrays Jewish lesbian author Gertrude Stein in pictures called *Chairman Ma*. Kass also gives the Warhol screen print treatment to herself, her grandmother, and *The Jewish Jackie*, a young Streisand in profile.

Kass was preoccupied with Warhol's style throughout the 1990s, and from 1999 to 2001 her traveling exhibition, "Deborah

Kass, The Warhol Project," was seen in cities across the United States. Billing her work as "Feel Good Paintings For Feel Bad Times,"[67] Kass's work humorously explores gender, ethnicity, and sexual identity. In doing so, she personalizes Warhol's style in a way that the pop artist never did.

Colors, Shapes, and Images of Signs

While Kass utilizes the time-consuming screen printing process in her art, advanced digital technology has made art appropriation a much simpler process. Artist Benjamin Edwards uses that technology to appropriate the mundane imagery people are exposed to every time they drive down a busy street. In his earliest works, such as the 1996 *Gas and Fast Food Icons*, Edwards reproduced thirty-six business logos (identifying symbols) on two sheets of standard graph paper. He removed the company names, however. Viewers are left to discern which icons belong to Shell, Exxon, Texaco, Pizza Hut, Burger King, Diary Queen, and so on. The work demonstrates how recognizable these icons are without their identifying letters because they are such common images in the modern world. As Edwards writes, most people are simply passive observers in a world that treats them as nothing more than passive shoppers and consumers:

> Over the past several decades, the landscape has been transformed by the . . . needs of the automobile . . . [which] like television, a medium for advertising, [is] a funnel through pure consumption space. Travel through this space is cinematic, speed generating the projector: the colors, shapes, and images of signs, architecture, and billboards wash over and through the viewer. Through the frame of the windshield, landscapes, vistas, geometric compositions, and narratives unfold, approach, reach optimal visual display, then speed to peripheral view and recede into the rearview mirror to make way for the next presentation. The

driver is a passive receiver, a screen onto which visuals are projected.[68]

Edwards followed the icon work with the *Conglomerate* series, which includes dozens of wordless gas station logos layered upon one another. The most impressive painting of the series, also called *Conglomerate*, is a huge 6-by-9-foot canvas (1.8m by 2.7m). It was created by the artist when he laid the building designs and logos from forty-five national chain stores one upon the other. The painting seems to explode with the reds, yellows, oranges, blues, and greens associated with the distinctive designs of Borders, Home Depot, McDonalds, and Starbucks. The look of *Conglomerate*, according to Simon Watson on Artnet, is "an image of a single theme-park esthetic super-store, a utopia for euphoric consumerism where you can buy anything and everything."[69]

Edwards uses a laborious process to appropriate chain store logos. He visits each site, photographs the stores inside and out, writes field notes, and makes dozens of drawings, called *Experiences*, that include distinctive designs such as the red roof of a KFC.

The artist's technique has changed over time. In the mid-1990s he used a traditional camera with slide film to photograph his sites. The slides were then projected onto a canvas one by one, allowing Edwards to trace and paint them in hard-edged acrylic paint before projecting another image.

Computer graphics technology has changed the way Edwards works. He now takes digital photos of sites and layers them together into virtual models using 3D modeling software. This has allowed the artist to create realistic three-dimensional worlds such as *We, The Wanderer*, and *Hidden Village*. With lone ghostly figures floating through entirely artificial worlds constructed by multinational corporations, the artist's imagery is a discomforting glimpse into the world of the future.

Commenting on his inspiration for the unique paintings, Edwards writes: "What will [the] capitalist vision look like in 100 years? In 1,000 years? I like to think of the world I'm trying to paint as one imagined from the eyes of an artist as far from our present situation as we are from ancient Rome."[70]

Cory Arcangel calls himself a hacker artist because he inserts popular images or icons into obsolete video game cartridges and computer software instead of using other conventional mediums for his work.

"A Savvy, Post-adolescent Hacker"

Computers have been useful tools for artists since they were first sold in the 1980s. While most use Photoshop or 3D software to manipulate images, Cory Arcangel is unique among appropriation artists. Arcangel reprograms obsolete video game cartridges and computer software systems. He is among the few appropriators who call themselves hacker artists. As with so much other appropriation art, Andy Warhol makes an appearance in Arcangel's work.

For the videogame *I Shot Andy Warhol*, which can be seen on YouTube, Arcangel reprogrammed "Hogan's Alley," a 1980s Ninetendo video game. The artist inserted pop-up cartoon images of Warhol along with other well-known icons such as a pope figure, Colonel Sanders, and rap star Flavor Flav. Arcangel chose these characters because they could be made recognizable within the poor resolution of the primitive, 8-bit video game. For example, Warhol is identified by his trademark bouncy blond wig.

When Arcangel first exhibited *I Shot Andy Warhol* in 2002, players sat on soft sofas and shot at their targets with plastic guns rather than playing the game with joysticks. After viewing Arcangel's unique art at the 2004 Armory Show in New York City, critic John Haber wrote:

SUPER MARIO MOVIE

Hacker artist Cory Arcangel created the fifteen-minute Super Mario Movie *from a 1980s Ninetendo Entertainment Systems (NES) video game. Game designer Matt Hawkins describes the plot of* Super Mario Movie *on the Game Set Watch Web site:*

The "movie" features Mario traversing his familiar fantastical haunts, but things are indeed falling apart, with all the graphics and even the sounds messed up. Everything is meant to illustrate a video game world that's deteriorating due to age (and the result is not that different from booting up an old NES game that needs to be removed from the system). . . . Events are loosely tied together via broken game speak, reminiscent of the good old days of bad translations.

At a certain point, Mario comes across a blue Goomba [a brown mushroom-like creature] and is taken to . . . a rave. The true highlight of the movie, the rave scene isn't brilliant due to the concept but in its execution; the action is a bit hard to describe, though I will say it's more [like the video game] Pong than Mushroom Kingdom . . . and Mario being merged with some other game, one that is relatively primitive, is rather fascinating on a historical and metaphysical level, and makes [one] wonder…[about] Mario's place in "the order of things." . . . The important thing to know is that the piece does an excellent job of playing with and adding some meaning behind one's conceptions of "messed up" graphics, with the most effective moment behind the long pause in the action at a certain point, which makes [one] wonder if the game had crashed (perhaps it almost did for real).

Matt Hawkins, "COLUMN: 'Cinema Pixeldiso' — Super Mario Movie(s)," *Game Set Watch*, October 20, 2006. www.gamesetwatch.com/2006/10/column_cinema_pixeldiso_super.php.

"I Shot Andy Warhol," his arcade game that allows people to take aim at pop-up cartoons of the master of replicas himself, seemed to have everything going for it. It had an ear for the art world and its media icons, a hacker's distrust of copyright law, a politically incorrect license to kill in the name of digital art, and the viewer's—no, make that the player's—eager involvement every step of the way. In other words, it clung to the right illusions and had all the right targets. It suggests a savvy, post-adolescent hacker fondly recalling the technology and culture of his childhood. Nintendo and other early games are back . . . as an unending cartoon road into a distant nowhere.[71]

Arcangel has also created hacks from the Super Mario Brothers (SMB) cartridges, which revolutionized video gaming when first introduced in 1985. *Super Mario Clouds* is a hacked SMB cartridge with all the graphics erased except for the clouds. For the *Super Mario Movie* Arcangel produced a fifteen-minute movie using only images from the SMB cartridge to tell a story. Arcangel described the plot as, "Mario's world falling apart. Like [the film] Mad Max, but in 8 bits."[72]

Making People Think

From Duchamp's toilet to SMB cartridges, modern society continues to flood the world with consumer goods for every need. These provide fodder for appropriation artists who use them to evoke feelings of nostalgia, humor, fear, prejudice, and human yearning.

Throughout the ages the goal of art has been to make people think. Although appropriation artists use pirated images instead of brush and paint, little doubt exists that their pieces are thought provoking and generate controversy among critics and the public.

5

Neo-Expressionism

In 1965 eighty-four-year-old Pablo Picasso created a series of roughly executed paintings in garish colors filled with emotional imagery. Many of the paintings featured coarsely rendered phalluses, breasts, and human bodies intertwined in love. Reviewers dismissed these paintings as "pornographic fantasies of an impotent old man, or the slapdash works of an artist who was past his prime,"[73] according to Belgian art critic Bruno Dillen. It was not until several years after Picasso's 1973 death that critics realized the artist had invented a new style, neo-Expressionism.

In the 1980s Picasso's style of expressing aggressive feelings with frenzied brushwork strongly influenced artists in the United States and sparked "a renaissance of American painting,"[74] according to Sandler. The neo-Expressionist movement was also taking root on the other side of the Atlantic ocean. In Italy, the genre was referred to as *transavantgarde* (beyond avant-garde), and in Germany practitioners of the style were called *Neue Wilden*, or the new wild ones. These painters had once again elevated the importance of depicting human figures in ways that reflected "the artists' state of mind rather than the reality of the external world,"[75] according to art scholar Nicolas Pioch on WebMuseum, Paris.

Like most new art styles, neo-Expressionism was a reaction against something, in this case a reaction against appropriation, installations, and conceptual art. The new wave of painters saw these forms of postmodernism as emotionless, cold, and calculating. Artistic skills with brush and paint were unimportant to those wishing to make political and cultural statements with found art, obscure concepts, or clever installations. Neo-Expressionism rose in popularity, according to critic Kay Larson, because, artists "are desperate to reconnect with feeling. . . . There is a compulsion to *make [emotional] contact*—whether with materials, or with the heroic possibilities of painting, or with the myth of the artist-creator, dormant during twenty-odd years of irony and intellectual distance in art."[76]

Expressionism and Abstract Expressionism

Neo-Expressionism means new expressionism, and the genre is based on the expressionist movement that developed in northern Europe in the early twentieth century. Norwegian painter Edvard Munch is one of the founders of the movement, and his 1893 painting *The Scream* is one of its most famous examples. *The Scream* depicts a simply drawn, almost skeletal figure standing on a bridge with his mouth wide open and his hands covering his ears. The sky is a swirling turmoil of orange, red, blue, and aqua green. Although the figure appears to be screaming, he is actually in a panic to cover his ears so as not to hear what Munch described as "a great unending scream piercing through nature."[77]

Munch did most of his work in Berlin, and the pain, despair, and alienation depicted in *The Scream* inspired the school of German expressionism. Like Munch, German expressionists such as Ernst Ludwig Kirchner rendered figures in clashing colors with distorted forms and features. This sort of slashing, fierce, emotional painting method was later adopted by Jackson Pollock and other founders of the abstract expressionist movement. Both the expressionists and the abstract expressionists inspired neo-Expressionism. As Sandler writes, "The neo-expressionists wanted

The Expressionist Bridge

Neo-Expressionism was inspired by the German expressionist movement called The Bridge founded in the early twentieth century. Art scholar Nicolas Pioch describes the movement and its creators on WebMuseum, Paris:

Die Brücke (The Bridge) was the first of two Expressionist movements that emerged in Germany in the early decades of the twentieth century. In 1905 a group of German Expressionist artists came together in Dresden and took that name . . . to indicate their faith in the art of the future, towards which their work would serve as a bridge. In practice they were not a cohesive group, and their art became an angst-ridden type of Expressionism. . . . Ernst Ludwig Kirchner (1880–1938), the leading spirit of Die Brücke . . . insisted that the group, which included Erich Heckel (1883–1970) and Karl Schmidt-Rottluf (1884–1976), "express inner convictions . . . with sincerity and spontaneity." They used images of the modern city to convey a hostile, alienating world, with distorted figures and colors. Kirchner does just this in *Berlin Street Scene* (1913), where the shrill colors and jagged hysteria of his own vision flash forth uneasily. There is a powerful sense of violence, contained with difficulty, in much of their art.

Nicolas Pioch, "Expressionism," WebMuseum, Paris, October 14, 2002. www.ibiblio.org/wm/paint/tl/20th/expressionism.html.

Ernst Ludwig Kirchner's Berlin Street Scene, *1913, is one of the most famous pieces of Die Brücke art.*

The Scream painted by Norwegian artist Edvard Munch in 1893 is one of the most famous examples of Expressionist art.

to paint directly—even instinctively—thereby continuing the tradition of historic expressionism."[78]

The Spirit of the Times

Neo-Expressionist painters began portraying the human body and other recognizable objects in Europe in the early 1980s. In England two important exhibitions featuring the new style of figurative painting were held at the Royal Academy in London.

In 1981 the exhibition *A New Spirit in Painting* featured mostly German painters, as did *Zeitgeist* ("The Spirit of the Times") which followed a year later. The 1981 exhibition was remarkable for two reasons. The display featured what curator Norman Rosenthal called "great painting . . . produced today . . . [and] a manifesto and . . . reflection on the state of painting now."[79] It was also the first major exhibition of international contemporary painting anywhere in Europe since 1965.

Still Life, 1976–1977, was created by Georg Baselitz, a leading pioneer of the German neo-Expressionist movement.

The new painting represented what Rosenthal called "human experiences . . . people and their emotions, landscapes, and still-lives."[80] Cocurator Christos M. Joachimides explained that the artists in the exhibition wanted to tell patrons about "personal relationships and personal worlds. . . . It is the need to talk about oneself, to express one's own desires and fears, to react to daily life . . . areas of experience that have long lain dormant."[81] This desire for personal expression through rough, violent painting would be the hallmark of neo-Expressionism for the remainder of the decade.

Georg Baselitz, born near Dresden in 1938, is considered a leading pioneer of German neo-Expressionism. His style of depicting figures in a wild, brutal manner was undoubtedly inspired by personal events in his life. His first memories are of Nazism and coming of age under repressive East German communism after World War II ended in 1945. His first paintings in 1964 were coarsely rendered depictions of what Sandler calls "hulking, loutish peasants, herdsmen and hunters with their genitals exposed, all roaming the smoldering rubble of [postwar] Germany."[82] This work was referred to as psychotic art because Baselitz was inspired by art produced by the mentally ill.

Baselitz moved to West Berlin in the early 1960s and continued to create figures in a deranged manner. For example, the 1975 *Male Nude* is shown upside down, and the method in which it is rendered is startling. According to the North Carolina Museum of Art: "The image seems almost hacked into being: paint is brushed, scratched, scraped and smeared with the fingers. What results is not a pretty picture but a haunting, even poignant, image of a human being alone and naked in the late 20th century."[83]

The Sound of Violent Human Tragedy

By 1980 Baselitz had established his reputation, and exhibitions of his work appeared in cities across the globe. This created a hunger for neo-Expressionist paintings among American art consumers who were tired of the intellectual, introverted, abstract, and remote art of the seventies. In New York, neo-Expressionists Julian Schnabel, David Salle, and Jean-Michel Basquiat found their work in great demand. They were able to rise to prominence as a result of aggressive marketing by galleries and art dealers.

Although Julian Schnabel was one of the best-selling artists during the early 1980s, his broken-plate paintings were often criticized by art reviewers.

Schnabel burst upon the art world in 1979 with large paintings whose surfaces were covered with broken plates and jagged pieces of crockery. For the next two years Schnabel painted figures with gruesome veins and scars on canvases littered with broken plates. These shards expressed shock, anger, and turmoil, according to Schnabel: "[The] sound of glass breaking or plates breaking call to mind parents fighting or . . . screaming. . . . The plates seemed to have a sound, the sound of every violent human tragedy. . . . I wanted to make something that was exploding as much as I wanted to make something that was cohesive."[84]

Schnabel returned art to its most basic form of visual expression, and he quickly became the most talked-about artist in New York. In 1982 alone he had eight solo exhibitions and participated in twenty-two group showings. His paintings were selling for $71,000 in 1982 (which is the equivalent of $150,000 today), but he was widely criticized by art reviewers. As Robert Hughes wrote in *Time*, "Schnabel is immensely fashionable with collectors for reasons the work does not make clear."[85]

Despite the criticism, Schnabel continued to depict figures in a controversial manner. In the 1983 *Vita*, the artist painted a nude woman on a cross. The painting is described by art historian W.S. Di Piero in *Out of Eden: Essays on Modern Art*:

> [The] central figure is a crucified woman; the pieces of shattered plates that frame her emerge from the painting's

The Strategy of the Soul

When neo-Expressionists began to exhibit paintings in the early 1980s, they upset postmodernist purists who believed painting was dead. Critics, called "enemies of painting," believed the works of Julian Schnabel and David Salle were disreputable because of their commercial value to galleries, museums, and collectors. While some believed that the neo-Expressionists had "sold out" for a profit, curator Diego Cortez defended the work both for its commercial value and its artistic worth:

[D]espite] its layers of materialism, opportunism, and ambition, [the market supports] the most significant art of this time. To the critics who feel this new painting is mere marketing strategy, let me say that they are only partially correct. It is good marketing in bed with the best art. It is, I maintain, a strategy of the soul.

My admiration and respect for the new dealers who have supposedly "manipulated" and "packaged" this new art . . . is at least equal to that of the artists and their work.

Diego Cortez, *The Pressure to Paint.* New York: Marlborough Gallery, 1982, p. 5.

surface like star bursts, and some of the stellar debris tumbles into the configuration of the body itself. The fusion of oil pigment and jagged, rippling plate fragments makes the image look at once muscular and dismantled. The figure has a high, intense resolution even while it seems about to disintegrate. Formally, the painting is brilliant; conceptually, however, its presentation of the suffering female seems calculated to win sympathy (or approval) by virtue of its correct political tone.[86]

Moving away from the broken-plate paintings, Schnabel began painting biblical and classically themed subjects on black velvet. Once again, the artist gained notoriety for creating what some called bad art. Velvet is commonly used for garish portraits of fifties rock singer Elvis Presley or tacky depictions of dogs playing cards. The subject matter—large portraits of his dog or obscene words—was also described as taboo and in bad taste.

One Thing Calls Up Another

The work of David Salle is often associated with Schnabel because the two painters are friends and found acclaim around the same time. While both paint in the neo-Expressionist style, however, their work is very different. Schnabel is known for heroic, biblical, and classical imagery. Salle's figures are often appropriated from photographs. These are culled from a variety of sources, including his own black-and-white pictures, news photos, cartoon characters, magazines, pornography, ads from the 1950s, and "how to draw" manuals. These images, gathered together on a single canvas and placed in separate rectangular boxes, are often unrelated. For example, the 1985 *Muscular Paper* consists of three large panels. On the left panel, an abstract sculpture is painted in dark bluish gray. A reclining nude is superimposed on this image, painted in a bright orange outline. The center panel shows a rear view of two female nudes skipping rope, sketched in charcoal. This image was appropriated from a 1930s German film. Meanwhile, a leering, blue-faced Joker with bright red lips, taken from an equally dated Batman comic strip, is overpainted on the women's buttocks. An orange fountain is painted between and over these images. The right panel consists of a piece of blue and green plaid material overlaid with an image pirated from a 1922 painting, *Iron Bridge in Frankfurt*, by Max Beckmann. This image is said to be a tribute to the school of Die Brücke, or The Bridge painters, who were the founders of German expressionism at the beginning of the twentieth century.

Muscular Paper and similar paintings reveal Salle as a master of juxtaposition. He says he uses this method because he is unable to commit to a single subject. And multiple images can be used the same way a composer employs many notes to create chords in a song. As Salle explains:

> I start with an inability to see things singularly. The idea that you could muster the necessary belief in a mark or a shape to let that be the carrier of all the

Neo-Expressionist painter David Salle often uses several seemingly unrelated images in just one piece of art. Critics claim that as a result, Salle's art represents nothing.

artistic meaning doesn't work for me. One thing automatically calls up another thing. And then that rhyme calls up a third thing to make a kind of chord. I have a musical analogy in mind.[87]

Many of Salle's critics do not see his paintings this way. Some are puzzled because the images are unrelated and arbitrary and therefore represent nothing. Others have accused Salle of sexism for his use of scantily clad women in suggestive poses. For example, reviewer Mira Schor stated that Salle's imagery seems "to be a continuation of a male conversation which is centuries old, to which women are irrelevant except as depersonalized projections of man's fears and fantasies."[88] Salle responds by pointing out that his paintings, in some ways, resemble television commercials where sexy models might be juxtaposed with banal images of beer cans and pickup trucks. Therefore, Salle's fragmented images offer a commentary on the postmodern world that capitalizes on primal urges in order to sell products. In the artist's own words, "Like, ho, ho, maybe we really are morally bankrupt. And maybe it's fun."[89]

A "Crazy Kid from Brooklyn"

In true neo-Expressionist style, Salle created his images quickly, letting his feelings, not his intellect, guide his hand. But few painters of the era could match the emotional impact of Jean-Michel Basquiat, whose primitive images flowed fast and furious as the painter rocketed to international stardom.

Basquiat did not attend art school but rather honed his craft as a graffiti artist on the streets of Brooklyn. Born in 1960 to a Haitian father and an American-born Puerto Rican mother, Basquiat grew up in a middle-class home and strongly identified with African American or Afrocentric culture. He attracted attention with his partner Al Diaz, writing puzzling phrases on New York buildings and signing them SAMO, for "Same Old [Stuff]."[90] His tags featured taunting lines such as "SAMO as a neo art form," "SAMO as an end to mindwash religion, nowhere politics and bogus philosophy," and "SAMO as an end to playing art."[91]

According to art historian Robert Rosenblum, Basquiat was a "crazy kid from Brooklyn who . . . began his meteoric career by raucously embracing a counter-cultural life, living in public parks, selling painted T-shirts on the street, [and] spraying graffiti on city walls."[92] Although Basquiat's graffiti seemed randomly applied, it most often appeared near trendy art galleries in the SoHo district. By 1982 Basquiat had become a fixture on the SoHo art scene, playing in a "noise" band called Gray, which performed at punk clubs such as CBGB and the Mudd Club. During this time he dated the then-unknown singer Madonna. Meanwhile, he was creating neo-Expressionist paintings with scribbled words and graffiti, images from his life, pop culture references, and scenes from black and Hispanic history.

After a 1980 show in an alternative Lower East Side gallery, Basquiat was discovered by an art agent who brought him nearly instant success. The twenty-year-old artist's highly marketable style attacked middle-class culture and was often painted on unusual media, such as broken refrigerators and other items retrieved from junkyards. Although Basquiat's images were antimaterialism and antiestablishment, according to Basquiat.com, "he came to personify the art scene of the 80s, with its merging of youth culture, money, hype, excess, and self-destruction."[93] He took huge quantities of cocaine, used a garbage can lid for a paint palette, and often painted while dressed in thousand-dollar Armani suits which he later wore in public, splattered with paint.

The Grand Spectacle

The artist's drug-fueled paranoia and excessive behavior often overshadowed his work. Basquiat's Afrocentric art, however, was unique in the 1980s. As art curator Kellie Jones states, "people weren't talking about Black or Latino cultures in the way [they do now]. In 1983 he was really ahead of his time."[94]

Basquiat was a jazz fanatic with over three thousand records. Jazz musicians such as Miles Davis, Dizzy Gillespie, and especially saxophonist Charlie Parker are featured promi-

Even after artist Jean-Michel Basquiat's tragic death in 1988, people continued to make money from his artwork. Basquiat's piece titled *Profit I* sold for more than $5.5 million in 2002.

nently in his work. Other figures include his political heroes, such as Malcolm X and Marcus Garvey, and sports figures Jesse Owens and Sugar Ray Robinson.

The crudely drawn 1982 work *CPRKR* (Charlie Parker) is typical of Basquiat's early style. The work, which resembles a

A Reputation for High Living

Several weeks after Jean-Michel Basquiat died at the age of twenty-seven in August 1988, the New York Times *ran the following article about his career, his life, and his death:*

[Jean-Michel] Basquiat was the most famous of only a small number of young black artists who have achieved national recognition. . . . While Mr. Basquiat outwardly enjoyed the life of an artistic and social prodigy, he was viewed by many friends, art dealers and critics as ill-starred.

Some say he resented being a black man whose fate twisted with the whims of an all-white jury of artistic powers. Others say he pined for fame but was crushed by its burdens. Some friends believe greedy art dealers and collectors exploited him. Some say wealth fed his longtime appetite for drugs. . . .

Mr. Basquiat rapidly earned a reputation for high living. He staged lush parties with giant video screens and catered food, treated crowds to dinners at expensive restaurants, and flew friends to the West Coast for weekends. He painted in designer suits that were usually splattered with colors by the time a work was completed.

Much of the money also went to friends and strangers—Bowery bums to whom he gave $100 bills, and struggling artists who got free paints and canvas. . . . Keith Haring, another graffiti artist who became successful, said Mr. Basquiat's extravagant spending on food and travel was his "way of sticking your nose up at people who were looking down on you."

Michael Wines, "Jean Michel Basquiat: Hazards of Sudden Success and Fame," *New York Times*, August 27, 1988. http://query.nytimes.com/gst/fullpage.html?res=940DE7D71E3DF934A1575BC0A96E948260&sec=&spon=&partner=permalink&exprod=permalink.

Jean-Michel Basquiat was one of only a few black artists to gain national attention during the 1980s. His artistic career was cut short when he died of a drug overdose at the age of twenty-seven.

tombstone, is painted on a piece of canvas tacked on tied wood supports. Brown paint is roughly smeared around the edges and the words "CPRKR STANHOPE HOTEL APRIL SECOND NINETEEN FIFTY ~~THREE~~ FIVE" are written on the work. (The word THREE is crossed out and replaced below with FIVE). This alludes to Parker's death from a heroin overdose at the Stanhope on April 2, 1955.

An image of a crown appears beneath the letters CPRKR. Basquiat included the crown as a mark of respect, indicating that Parker was part of a royal family. The sax player is also referred to as Charles the First at the bottom. Other images appear to be blotted out with smears of black paint. Commenting on the work, Basquiat stated: "Since I was seventeen, I thought I might be a star. I'd think about all my heroes, Charlie Parker, Jimi Hendrix. . . . I had a romantic feeling of how people had become famous."[95]

By 1983 Basquiat had himself become world famous, with exhibitions in New York, California, Europe, and Japan. He continued to explore his cultural heritage with epic works such as *The Nile*, which connects his own American heritage with the history of the United States and ancient Africa. *The Nile* depicts slaves being transported to the Americas aboard a ship, while several African masks are painted on one side of the work. The phrase "el gran espectáculo" (the grand spectacle) stretches across the top, an ironic commentary on a shameful centuries-long tragedy. Other imagery and words in the work allude to ancient Egypt, the early civilization along the Nile that provided a basis of African American culture, according to the artist.

Basquiat created many more monumental paintings in 1983 including, *Notary* and *Undiscovered Genius of the Mississippi Delta*. All explore Basquiat's heritage, cultural identity, heroes, and themes of justice and equality. The young painter's talent and fame brought him to the attention of Andy Warhol, and the artists collaborated on several works. The 1985 *Arm and Hammer II* combines typical elements of both artists. The logo from the baking soda box is faithfully reproduced twice by Warhol while the image on the left features Basquiat's cartoonish Charlie Parker blowing on a saxophone while the year of his death is written below. Other works such as *Zenith ad* and *GE logo* were not well received by critics.

When Warhol died in 1987 Basquiat became extremely distraught, and his drug intake increased to include heroin, cocaine, amphetamines, depressants, and alcohol. Hovering on the verge of insanity, Basquiat continued to paint, but critics became increasingly unkind, saying he was only repeating themes and images from his earlier works. On August 12, 1988, Basquiat died at the age of twenty-seven from an overdose of heroin and cocaine. His last painting, appropriately titled *Riding with Death*, is a simple drawing of a black and brown death figure riding a horse skeleton. The horse's skull has crosses in its eye sockets. (*Horse* is a slang term for heroin).

Basquiat's death made some in the art world question the ethics of an industry that could encourage a young man's self-destruction while profiting from his madness. But even after his death, great sums were to be made. In 2002 Basquiat's sarcastically titled work *Profit I* was auctioned at New York's famous auction house Christie's for more than $5.5 million. The work was painted in Italy in 1982, when Basquiat was only twenty-one years old.

"Painters Will Paint"

Although neo-Expressionists were the most successful artists of the postmodern art era, the genre was never completely accepted by many art critics. For example, in 1981 critic Douglas Crimp stated that in the postmodern world, painting was dead and neo-Expressionists could not revive it. However, as Schnabel told interviewer Max Hollein in 2003, "The conversation about painting being dead has gone on for about one hundred years. People have been talking about the death of painting for so many years that most of the people are dead now. Painting is alive. . . . Painters will paint."[96]

Notes

Introduction: Beyond Modern Art

1. David Bates, "Beyond Postmodernism," LensCulture, 2005. www.lensculture.com/bate1.html.
2. Jonathan Selwood, *The Pinball Theory of the Apocalypse*. New York: Harper Perennial, 2007, p. 164.

Chapter 1: Roots of Postmodernism

3. Quoted in Wayne Clements, "A Pessimistic Mechanics?" In-Vacua.com, 2006. www.in-vacua.com/a_%20pessimistic_mechanics.html.
4. Quoted in MOMA, "Marcel Duchamp: Bicycle Wheel," 2007. www.moma.org/collection/printable_view.php?object_id=81631.
5. Quoted in MOMA, "Marcel Duchamp: Bicycle Wheel."
6. Quoted in Thomas McEvilley, *The Triumph of Anti-Art*. Kingston, NY: McPherson & Company, 2005, p. 23.
7. Leah Dickerman, *Dada*. Washington, DC: National Gallery of Art, 2006, p. 7.
8. Quoted in McEvilley, *The Triumph of Anti-Art*, p. 17.
9. MOMA, "The Collection," 2007. www.moma.org/collection/browse_results.php?object_id=37013.
10. Quoted in Dickerman, *Dada*, p. 158.
11. Quoted in Elizabeth Fisher, "Art About Nothing," *National Review Online*, March 31, 2006. www.nationalreview.com/comment/fisher200603310826.asp.
12. Electro-Acoustic Music, "Dadaism," 2007. www.camil.music.uiuc.edu/Projects/EAM/Dadaism.html.
13. Quoted in Marjorie Perloff, "Dada Without Duchamp/Duchamp Without Dada," Electronic Poetry Center, 1998. http://epc.buffalo.edu/authors/perloff/dada.html.
14. Quoted in Binghamton University Department of Art History, "Fountain," October 17, 2007. http://arthist.binghamton.edu/duchamp/fountain.html.
15. Art Science Research Laboratory, "L.H.O.O.Q." 2006. www.marcelduchamp.net/L.H.O.O.Q.php.
16. Quoted in University of Exeter, "Where Dada Stands in History," 2007. www.spa.ex.ac.uk/drama/dada/page4.html.

17. Quoted in Jeffery Brown, "Jackson Pollock," Online News Hour, PBS, January 11, 1999. www.pbs.org/newshour/bb/entertainment/jan-june99/pollock_1-11.html.
18. Quoted in The Slide Projector, "Is He the Greatest Living Painter in the United States?" 2006. www.theslideprojector.com/art1/art1primarysources/1949lifearticle.html.
19. Metropolitan Museum of Art, "Robert Rauschenberg Combines," 2007. www.metmuseum.orgspecial/Rauschenberg/view_1.asp?item=0&view=l.
20. Michael Kimmelman, "Art Out of Anything: Rauschenberg in Retrospect," *New York Times*, December 23, 2006. www.nytimes.com/2005/12/23/arts/design/23raus.html.
21. Quoted in "Jasper Johns," *American Masters*, PBS, 2006. www.pbs.org/wnet/americanmasters/database/johns_j.html.
22. Quoted in Time-Life Books, *Turbulent Years: The 60s*. Alexandria, VA: Time-Life Books, 1998, p. 42.
23. The Andy Warhol Homepage, "The Andy Warhol Biography." www.warhol.dk.

Chapter 2: Conceptual Art

24. Ursula Meyer, *Conceptual Art*. New York: E.P. Dutton, 1972, p. vii.
25. Quoted in Michael Kimmelman, "Sol LeWitt, Master of Conceptualism, Dies at 78," *New York Times*, April 9, 2007. www.nytimes.com/2007/04/09/arts/design/09lewitt.html?_r=5&oref=slogin&oref=slogin&oref=slogin&oref=slogin&oref=login.
26. Quoted in Michael Delahunt, "Conceptual Art," Artlex, 2007. www.artlex.com/ArtLex/c/conceptualart.html.
27. Michael Delahunt, "Artlex's Con Page," Artlex, 2007. www.artlex.com/ArtLex/Con.html#anchor45118.
28. Henry Flynt, "Henry Flynt's Concept Art," Radical Art, 2007. http://radicalart.info/concept/flynt.html.
29. Quoted in Gregory Battock, ed., *Idea Art: A Critical Anthology*. New York: E.P. Dutton, 1973, p. 176.
30. Henry Flynt, "Henry Flynt Philosophy," 2007. www.henryflynt.org/overviews/hfphotos.html.
31. McEvilley, *The Triumph of Anti-Art*, p. 65.
32. Quoted in McEvilley, *The Triumph of Anti-Art*, p. 61.
33. Quoted in *Time*, "All Package," 2007. www.time.com/time/magazine/article/0,9171,838942-2,00.html.
34. David Bourdon, "MOCA Wrapped," Christo and Jeanne-Claude, 2007. www.christojeanneclaude.net/moca.shtml.
35. Quoted in Werner Hammerstingl, "Installation Art: Christo's Reichstag," olinda.com, 1998. www.olinda.com/ArtAndIdeas/lectures/christo.htm.
36. Yoko Ono, "Yoko Ono One-Flux-film 14 - 1966.flv," Multiplicity, 2008.

http://hninh.multiply.com/video/item/7.

37. Yoko Ono, "Selected Instruction Pieces by Yoko Ono," a-i-u.net, 2007. www.a-i-u.net/instructions.html.
38. Quoted in Reiko Tomii and Kathleen M. Friello, *Yes Yoko Ono*. New York: Harry N. Abrams, 2000, p. 28.
39. Tomii and Friello, *Yes Yoko Ono*, p. 190.

Chapter 3: Installation Art

40. Mark Rosenthal, *Understanding Installation Art*. Munich: Prestel, 2003, pp. 26–27.
41. Rosenthal, *Understanding Installation Art*, p. 26.
42. Rosenthal, *Understanding Installation Art*, p. 27.
43. Claire Bishop, *Installation Art*. New York: Routledge, 2005, p. 23.
44. Quoted in Bishop, *Installation Art*, p. 23.
45. Quoted in Bishop, *Installation Art*, p. 23.
46. Quoted in Jeff Kelly, *Childsplay: The Art of Allan Kaprow*. Berkeley: University of California Press, 2004, p. 71.
47. Quoted in John Held Jr., "An Interview with Allan Kaprow," November 23, 2001. www.geocities.com/johnheldjr/InterviewWithAlanKaprow.html.
48. Irving Sandler, *Art in the Postmodern Era*. New York: Icon Editions, 1996, p. 114.
49. Quoted in Sandler, *Art in the Postmodern Era*, p. 118.
50. Carrie Mae Weems, "Womanhouse," Feminist Art, December 19, 2007. http://feministartrevolution.blogspot.com/2007/12/womanhouse-1973.html.
51. Brooklyn Museum, "The Dinner Party: Place Setting: Sojourner Truth," April 13, 2007. www.brooklynmuseum.org/eascfa/dinner_party/place_settings/sojourner_truth.php.52. Bishop, *Installation Art*, p. 37.
53. PBS, "tropos," *Art: 21*, 2007. www.pbs.org/art21/artists/hamilton/card3.html.
54. Bishop, *Installation Art*, p. 82.
55. PBS, "Atlan," *Art: 21*, 2007. www.pbs.org/art21/artists/turrell/card1.html.
56. Bishop, *Installation Art*, p. 87.

Chapter 4: Appropriation Art

57. Quoted in Scott McLemee, "Stolen Words," Inside Higher Ed, January 26, 2006. www.insidehighered.com/views/2006/01/25/mclemee.
58. Quoted in Sandler, *Art in the Postmodern Era*, p. 386.
59. MOMA, "Sherrie Levine: After Walker Evans: 2," 2007. www.metmuseum.org/toah/hd/pcgn/hod_1995.266.2.htm.
60. Quoted in Rosetta Brooks, *Richard Prince*. New York: Whitney Museum of American Art, 1992, p. 85.

61. Quoted in Brooks, *Richard Prince*, p. 130.
62. Guggenheim Museum, "Richard Prince: Spiritual America," September 2007. www.guggenheim.org/exhibitions/exhibition_pages/prince. html.
63. Monica Racic, "You Are Not Yourself: A Glimpse into the Work of Barbara Kruger," *d/visible*, April 5, 2007. http://dvisible.com/?p=223.
64. Quoted in Russell Fergusen et al., eds., *Discourses: Conversations in Postmodern Art and Culture*. Cambridge, MA: MIT Press, 1990, p. 198.
65. Quoted in Daisy Garnett, "Making a Scene," Damien Loeb's Unofficial Website, 2007. www.damianloeb.com/history/tm982001.html.
66. Richard Klein, "Homecoming," Damien Loeb's Unofficial Website, 2007. http://damianloeb.com/history/homecoming.html.
67. Deborah Kass, "The Warhol Project," 2008. www.deborahkass.com.
68. Benjamin Edwards, "The Rational Services the Romantic," Benjamin Edwards: Works, Projects, Archive, 1997. www.benjaminedwards.net/Writings/thesis2.htm.
69. Simon Watson, "Simon Says: Collect," Artnet, September 24, 1999. www.artnet.com/magzine_pre2000/news/watson/watson9-24-99.asp.
70. Benjamin Edwards, "The Origins of the Republic," Benjamin Edwards: Works, Projects, Archive, 2005. www.benjaminedwards.net/Writings/origins%20of%20republic.htm.
71. John Haber, "Cory Arcangel, Tim Hawkinson, and Charlotte Becket," New.York Art.Crit, May 19, 2004. www.haberarts.com/boytoys.htm#arcangel.
72. Quoted in Matt Hawkins, "'Cinema Pixeldiso'–Super Mario Movie(s)," Game Set Watch, October 20, 2006. www.gamesetwatch.com/2006/10/column_cinema_pixeldiso_super.php.

Chapter 5: Neo-Expressionism

73. Bruno Dillen, "Biography," Art in the Picture, 2005. http://artinthepicture.com/artists/Pablo_Picasso/biography.html.
74. Sandler, *Art in the Postmodern Era*, p. 222.
75. Nicolas Pioch, "Expressionism," WebMuseum, Paris, October 14, 2002. www.ibiblio.org/wm/paint/tl/20th/expressionism.html.
76. Kay Larson, "Art: Pressure Points," *New York*, June 28, 1982, p. 59.
77. Quoted in Tim Radford, "Stratospheric Echo Locates Munch's Scream," *Guardian*, December 10, 2003. http://arts.guardian.co.uk/news/story/0,11711,1103612,00.html.
78. Sandler, *Art in the Postmodern Era*, p. 223.
79. Christos M. Joachimides, Norman Rosenthal, and Nicholas Serota, *A New Spirit in Painting*. London: Royal Academy of Arts, p. 15.

80. Joachimides et al., *A New Spirit in Painting*, pp. 11–12.
81. Joachimides et al., *A New Spirit in Painting*, pp. 9–10.
82. Sandler, *Art in the Postmodern Era*, p. 309.
83. North Carolina Museum of Art, "Collections," 2008. www.ncartmuseum.org/collections/highlights/20thcentury/20th/1950-2000/baselitz_lrg.shtml.
84. Quoted in Sandler, *Art in the Postmodern Era*, p. 276.
85. Quoted in Sally Everett, ed., *Art Theory and Criticism*. Jefferson, NC: McFarland, 1991, p. 216.
86. W.S. Di Piero, *Out of Eden: Essays on Modern Art*. Berkeley: University of California Press, 1991, p. 209.
87. Artquotes.com, "David Salle Quotes," 2008.www.artquotes.net/masters/salle/david-quotes.htm.
88. Mira Schor, "Appropriating Sexuality," *M/E/A/N/I/N/G 1*, December 1986, p. 14.
89. Quoted in Sandler, *Art in the Postmodern Era*, p. 240.
90. Lenin Imports, "Jean-Michel Basquiat: Biography," June 2007. www.leninimports.com/basquiat_biog.html.
91. Artquotes.com, "Jean-Michel Basquiat Art Quotes," 2008. www.art quotes.net/masters/basquiat-quotes.htm.
92. Quoted in Lenny Campello, "Exhibition Review: Factory Work—Warhol, Wyeth, and Basquiat," BC Culture, October 5, 2006. http://blogcritics.org/archives/2006/10/05/065343.php.
93. Basquiat.com, "Home," 2004. www.basquiat.com.
94. Quoted in Tribe.net, "Jean-Michel Basquiat," February 18, 2006. http://afrolatindiaspora.tribe.net/thread/b26d10e0-7179-40b1-ae2f79cbbbf97c5c.
95. Jean-Michel Basquiat, "Street to Studio," Brooklyn Museum, 2007. www.brooklynmuseum.org/exhibitions/basquiat/street-to-studio/english/explore_heroes.php.
96. Quoted in Max Hollein, "Julian Schnabel Talks to Max Hollein—'80s Then—Interview," Artforum, April, 2003. http://findarticles.com/p/articles/mi_m0268/is_8_41/ai_10193858.

Glossary

appropriation: In postmodern art, the act of borrowing one creation and using it in a new way.

assemblage: A work of art made from a collection of different objects.

cubism: An artistic style pioneered by Pablo Picasso that represents natural forms as geometric shapes seen from several different angles at once.

Dada: An art movement based on the belief that the only sane reaction to the violence and madness of the modern world is to promote artistic anarchy with irrational statements and illogical anti-art.

expressionism: An art style that rejects objective reality and represents moods and feelings through distorted form and color.

installation: A three-dimensional art piece meant to stimulate the sense with objects, paintings, lights, sounds, videos, and so on.

modernism: The twentieth-century art movement that discarded traditional techniques practiced since the Renaissance, such as perspective, composition, and color.

neo-Expressionism: A style of modern painting where the human body is recognizable but portrayed in a violent, emotional way with vivid, garish colors.

postmodernism: A genre popular between the 1960s and 1990s in which artists embraced art forms such as commercials, magazines, and graphic arts and created works with new media such as garbage, electronics, and appropriated images.

surrealism: An art movement that sought to represent subconscious thought and dreams through odd juxtapositions, or contrasts, between reality and unusual forms.

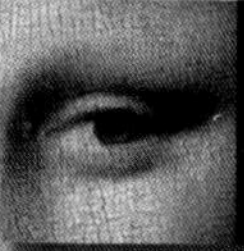

For Further Reading

Books

Jean-Michel Basquiat, *Basquiat*. Ed. Marc Mayer. New York: Brooklyn Museum, 2005. This book is a catalog from the 2005 exhibition at the Brooklyn Museum featuring the neo-Expressionist artwork of one of the most notable figures on the international art scene in the 1980s. Also includes essays by various art critics.

Jan Greenberg and Sandra Jordan, *Andy Warhol: Prince of Pop*. New York: Delacorte, 2004. This book charts the artist's rise from obscurity to his status as a pop icon and most famous proponent of pop art.

Jeff Kelley, *Childsplay: The Art of Allan Kaprow*. Berkeley and Los Angeles: University of California Press, 2004. Vivid descriptions and photos of the conceptual art "Happenings" Kaprow produced in the 1960s in which various art forms such as painting, music, and dance were turned into theatrical events.

Clare Oliver, *Jackson Pollock*. New York: Franklin Watts, 2003. Discusses the life, art, and legacy of the abstract expressionist known as Jack the Dripper, with his rise to fame, his place in art history, and the self-destructive behavior that led to his death.

Mark Rosenthal, *Understanding Installation Art*. Munich: Prestel, 2003. An exploration of installation art written by a museum curator, featuring dozens of full-color pictures of art installations created in the past century.

Julian Schnabel, *Julian Schnabel: Malerei/Paintings 1978–2003*. Ostfildern, Germany: Hatje Cantz, 2004. This volume presents a broad selection of Schnabel's large-scale, neo-Expressionist paintings with emphasis on works from 1990 to 2003.

Web Sites

Barbara Kruger.com (www.barbarakruger.com/index.php). A tribute to the American artist famous for her layered photographs that feature ironic, humorous, or tragic phrases which draw a contrast to the advertising images appropriated from magazines.

Christo and Jeanne-Claude (www.christojeanneclaude.net/moca.shtml). The homepage of the husband-wife team of conceptual artists famous for wrapping large buildings and natural sites in fabric. The couple's many projects from 1958 until the present day are discussed, and many photos are provided.

Damien Loeb's Unofficial Website (www.damianloeb.com). Art reproductions, interviews, biography, and other information concerning the American painter whose hyper-realistic paintings use appropriated images in juxtaposition with created imagery.

The Dinner Party: Place Settings (www.brooklynmuseum.org/eascfa/dinnerparty/place_settings/browse.php). A Brooklyn Museum Web site containing photos of all thirty-nine place settings on Judy Chicago's installation *The Dinner Party* dedicated to famous women throughout history. Each plate links to a page containing biographies of the women, detailed descriptions, and more photos of the place settings.

Marcel Duchamp World Community (www.marcelduchamp.net/L.H.O.O.php). This Web site of the Art Science Research Laboratory provides art reproductions, essays, interviews, and biographical and exhibition information concerning the man whose conceptual and appropriation art provided the foundation for postmodernism.

Yoko Ono: Imagine Peace (www.a-i-u.net). The homepage of renowned conceptual artist, author, and musician Yoko Ono. Features interviews with the artist, photos, and examples of her instruction art.

Index

Picture Credits

Cover: © Walter, Bieri/epa/Corbis
© 2008 Andy Warhol Foundation/ARS, New York/Trademarks, Campbell Soup Company. All rights reserved. Photo by Louisa Gouliamaki/AFP/Getty Images, 10
© 2008 Artists Rights Society (ARS), New York/ ADAGP, Paris. Photo by Olivier Laban-Mattei/AFP/Getty Images, 38
© 2008 Artists Rights Society (ARS), New York/ ADAGP/Paris/Succession Marcel Duchamp. Photo © The Museum of Modern Art/ Licensed by SCALA/Art Resource, NY, 16
© 2008 Artists Rights Society (ARS), New York/ VG Bild-Kunst, Bonn. Photo: The Museum of Modern Art/Licensed by SCALA/Art Resource/NY, 21
© 2008 The Estate of Jean-Michel Basquiat/ ADAGP, Paris/ARS, New York. Photo: Banque d'Images, ADAGP/Art Resource, NY, 95
© 2008 Judy Chicago/Artists Rights Society (ARS), New York. Photo by Stan Honda/ AFP/Getty Images, 59
© 2008 The Pollock-Krasner Foundation/Artists Rights Society (ARS), New York. Photo by Martha Holmes/Time & Life Pictures/Getty Images, 26
The Andy Warhol Foundation, Inc/Art Resource, NY. © 2000 Andy Warhol Foundation for the Visual Arts/ARS, NY, 31
The Art Archive/Museo/Bibliografico Musicale Bologna/Alfredo Dagli Orti/The Picture Desk, Inc., 51
Astrid Stawiarz/Getty Images, 75
Barbara Kruger work reproduced courtesy of Mary Boone Gallery, New York. Photo: © Boris Roessler/dpa/Corbis, 73
Baselitz, Georg (1938-) © Copyright. Still Life Stilleben, 1976-77. Oil on canvas, 8' 21/2 X 6' 67/8. Gift of Agnes Gund. (66.1991). Photo Credit: Digital Image © The Museum of Modern Art/Licensed by SCALA/Art Resource, NY The Museum of Modern Art, New York, NY, U.S.A., 87
Berlin Street Scene, 1913 (oil canvas), Kirchner, Ernst Ludwig (1880-1938)/Neue Galerie, New York, USA/The Bridgeman Art Library Art Credit: © by Ingeborg & Wolfgang Henze-Ketterer, Wichtrach/Bern, 85
Bryan Bedder/Getty Images, 46
© Christopher Felver/Corbis, 53, 65
Edvard Munch: The Scream 1910? Mixed medium on unprimed cardboard 83.5 x 66 cm Munch Museum, Oslo. © 2008 The Munch Museum/The Munch-Ellingsen Group/ Artists Rights Society (ARS), NY. Copyright photo: Munch Museum, 86
© H. Armstrong Roberts/Corbis, 11
© Jasper Johns/Licensed by VAGA, New York, NY. Photo by AP Images, 29
Kass, Deborah (b. 1952). Six Blue Barbras (The Jewish Jackie Series), 1992. Screen print and acrylic on canvas, 30 1/2 x 24 x 1 1/2 in. (77.5 x 61 x 3.8 cm). Gift of Seth Cohen, 2004–10. Photo by Richard Goodbody, Inc. The Jewish Museum, New York/Art Resource, NY, 77
Luciano Del Castillo/AFP/Getty Images, 34
© Marianne Haas/Corbis, 92
© The Museum of Modern Art/Licensed by Scala/Art Resource, NY. © 2008 Estate of Pablo Picasso/Artists Rights Society, New York, 14
Peter Kramer/Getty Images, 89
Photo: Wolfgang Volz, © Christo 1995, 43
Photo: Wolfgang Volz, © Christo and Jeanne-Claude 2005, 40
© Rose Hartman/Corbis, 96
Scott Wintrow/Getty Images, 80
Stan Honda/AFP/Getty Images, 57
Walker Evans/Hulton Archive/Getty Images, 68

About the Author

Stuart A. Kallen is the prolific author of more than 250 nonfiction books for children and young adults. He has written on topics ranging from the theory of relativity to the history of world music. In addition, Kallen has written award-winning children's videos and television scripts. In his spare time, he is a singer/songwriter/guitarist in San Diego, California.